JOHN F. KENNEDY

JOHN F. KENNEDY

Lois E. Anderson

LONGMEADOW
P R E S S

This 1992 edition published by
Longmeadow Press
201 High Ridge Road
Stamford CT 06904

Produced by
Brompton Books Corporation
15 Sherwood Place
Greenwich CT 06830

ISBN 0-681-41594-0

Printed in Hong Kong

0 9 8 7 6 5 4 3 2

Page 1: *President John F
Kennedy signs the order to
interdict weapons to Cuba: 23
October 1962.*
Previous pages: *JFK's
eloquence as a public speaker
grew with the years.*
This page: *In Berlin, June
1963.*

Contents

Foreword

John Fitzgerald Kennedy became the 35th President of the United States on 20 January 1961. At the age of 43, he was the youngest man to achieve the presidency by election. Less than three years later, he would be the youngest to die in office.

From the beginning Kennedy lived in a world of risks and challenges. A war hero and apparently the epitome of a physically active man, he actually suffered much of his life from severe disabilities. A Roman Catholic, he experienced some political opposition on religious grounds, but he neither compromised nor capitalized on this issue and became the first of his faith to become America's Chief Executive. Although he lacked a long and distinguished record in Congress, he was the first to win the highest office from a US Senate seat.

Kennedy's confidence in what America could do inspired the nation during his campaign for the presidency. When he was revealed as fallible, his country was disappointed. The debate over what he might have accomplished with a longer term in office was never to be resolved. When this young, confident, engaging and very human man was assassinated, the world was shocked, and in the aftermath, one thing emerged as certain: John F Kennedy would not disappear from the consciousness of his countrymen.

Above: *The young Jack Kennedy with his grandfather* *Fitzgerald (left) and his father, Joseph P Kennedy.*

Above: *At the Democratic National Convention in Chicago – 1952.*

Above right: *In the Oval Office shortly after the Cuban missile crisis of 1962.*

Top left: *In Mexico City, where he was warmly received in the summer of 1962.*
Above: *With his predecessor Dwight D Eisenhower early in 1961, the year Kennedy took office.*

Top: *At the America's Cup races in Newport during 1962.*
Center: *With his son and namesake at Hyannis Port in the summer of 1963.*

Above: *North Portico, the Capitol: 25 November 1963.*

'If You Can't Be Captain ...'

Joseph P and Rose Kennedy in
1931 with, from left, Bobby,
Jack, Kathleen, Jean, Patricia,
Rosemary, Eunice and Joe Jr.
Edward was born the
following year.

Above: *Mayor John F 'Honey Fitz' Fitzgerald with Edward Everett Hale (right), during Old Home Week celebrations in Boston in 1907. John Kennedy's maternal grandfather was elected Mayor of Boston in 1906, after an exuberant campaign that took him to every corner of the city's Irish Catholic North End. By that time he had already served three terms in Congress: ward politics was one of the few fields open to Boston's Irish immigrants, many of whom – like Fitzgerald's parents – had fled the potato famine of 1840.*

Opposite: *In back seat, from left, Vice-President Charles W Fairbanks, Josiah P Quincy and Mayor Fitzgerald at the conclusion of Boston's 1907 Old Home Week celebration.*

Left: *Mayor Fitzgerald, G White and the portly and genial President William H Taft. Fitzgerald had a penchant for entertaining visiting dignitaries on a lavish scale, including, on one occasion, Admiral Togo of Japan.*

John F Kennedy, born into an Irish-Catholic family of wealth on 29 May 1917, in Brookline, Massachusetts, was familiar with political life from the beginning. His mother wrote later that he had been rocked to political lullabies. Both of the grandfathers who contributed their names to the future president were deeply involved in Democratic politics. Boston elections then were fought tough and sometimes funny, with political workers knocking on tenement doors in the middle of the night to remind the awakened householder to vote – for the opposing candidate.

His mother, Rose Kennedy, was the petite and pretty daughter of John Francis Fitzgerald. Known as Honey Fitz, Fitzgerald was a charming, cocky, intelligent man who served in Congress for six years from 1894. But the job that really mattered to him was that of mayor of Boston, and by 1905 he was the first native-born Irish-American to hold that office. His daughter Rose, who often acted as his official hostess, was familiar with political affairs at an early age.

When Rose married Joseph P Kennedy in October 1914, it was rumored that Honey Fitz thought she could have done better. Joseph's father was Patrick Joseph Kennedy, Fitzgerald's sometime political adversary. Quiet and dignified, he was a no-nonsense type who had made a fortune as a saloon-keeper and with other business interests. 'P J' Kennedy as he was called, was active in Boston politics as a ward boss. He was five times a member of the Massachusetts House of Representatives and once a state senator.

PJ's son, Joseph, was hard-working like his father. His penchant for odd jobs and money-making schemes in his boyhood came not from a need for money – the Kennedys were well-off – but from a strongly competitive nature. By the time he graduated from Harvard, Joseph Kennedy already had a small nest egg from a Boston sight-seeing enterprise he had run with a friend. His plan was to become a million-

aire by the time he was 35. He was on his way at 25, having been elected a bank president by the Columbia Trust Company. Boston newspapers reported that Joe Kennedy was the youngest bank president in the state, if not in the country.

The couple's first home was a modest one, purchased for $6500. The young husband had to take out a loan for the down payment, but he soon repaid it. Within a year, the children began to arrive one after another: Joseph P, Jr in 1915, John F in 1917, Rosemary in 1918 and Kathleen in 1920. The rapidly growing Kennedy family moved then to a larger home in Brookline, where three more children were born: Eunice in 1921, Patricia in 1924 and Robert in 1925.

Opposite: *Rose Fitzgerald, 1911.*
Below: *Rose's father, Honey Fitz.*

Top right: *Joseph P Kennedy, 1912.*
Bottom right: *Joe's father, Patrick J Kennedy.*

JF Kennedy

Right: *Joseph P Kennedy Sr with Joe Jr, aged four, and John, aged two, in Brookline – 1919.*
Bottom right: *On a summer holiday in Nantasket, Joe Kennedy holds hs namesake (left) and John, the second of his four sons.*
Below: *An aristocratic-looking young Franklin Delano Roosevelt in 1919, when he was Assistant Secretary of the Navy. He and Joseph P Kennedy became acquainted during World War I, when Kennedy was an executive at the Fore River Shipyard, which produced three dozen destroyers in a record 27 months.*

The year Jack Kennedy was born, his father became assistant manager of the Fore River Shipyard of the Bethlehem Shipbuilding Corporation. True to character, he also established a cafeteria, the Victory Lunchroom, to serve the work force. He worked at the shipyard during World War I, when his energy as an executive pushed production to the delivery of 36 destroyers in 27 months. It was through this effort that he met the then Assistant Secretary of the Navy, Franklin Delano Roosevelt. Later, as President, Roosevelt would appoint Joseph P Kennedy United States Ambassador to the Court of St James in London.

Joseph Kennedy began speculating, successfully, on the New York Stock Exchange during World War I. By 1929 he had acquired enough capital to endow each of his children with a million-dollar trust fund. He pulled out of the stock market before it crashed that year, in an impressive display of financial acumen. In 1926 he had begun his association with the motion-picture industry, becoming president and chairman of the board of directors of Film Booking Offices of America. That year the Kennedys moved from Boston to New York City. Their first home was in the suburb of Riverdale, but by the time Jack Kennedy was 12 they had moved to Bronxville in Westchester County. His sister Jean was born in 1928, and he was almost 15 years old and away at prep school when his brother Edward was born, completing the family.

On the ocean side of Cape Cod, at Hyannis Port, Massachusetts, a big white summer house, later known as 'the Compound,' was bought by Joseph Kennedy for his large family. There was also a winter home by the ocean in fashionable Palm Beach, Florida. Although wealth brought nurses and governesses into the children's lives, they were never distant from their parents. Joe and Rose Kennedy were devoted to their children.

In the Boston suburb where Jack Kennedy spent his early childhood, his life was not very different from that of other boys. He wasn't above breaking rules and getting spanked for it. He was known for misplacing his belongings, with an absentmindedness he shared with his mother. With so many children tumbling about, it is easy to see why Rose Kennedy pinned notes to her dress and kept a file-card index on her children's illnesses.

Jack Kennedy and his brothers and sisters were encouraged to develop their talents: their father instilled in all his children his own competitive drive. Second best would not do. Winning, excelling, were

all-important. His admonition to them was, 'If you can't be captain, don't play.'

Jack Kennedy's time was filled with sports and family games as he grew up. At Hyannis Port, a Fourth of July softball game between the team of Kennedy children, called the Barefoots, and the other summer residents, was a tradition. Touch football, swimming, hiking and sailing in the family sailboats, the *Tenovus* and then the *Onemore*, were all joined enthusiastically by Jack, although he was not the natural athlete that his older brother Joe was. Joe was both an admired big brother and a rival. A simple bicycle race could lead, as it did one day, to a spectacular finish in which they crashed into each other head on. What happened to the bikes wasn't recorded, but Jack reportedly needed more than 20 stitches.

Although rivalry among the Kennedy children often bordered on the fierce, their loyalty to each other was unquestioned. Among themselves they could compete, but against the world they were united. Family misfortunes – and the Kennedys were to see many – were faced by a courageous closed circle. Jack's sister Rosemary, as her mother was to reveal much later, was born retarded, which was then viewed as a dire affliction for the whole family, with implications of possible failure in everyone. The Kennedy family took up the care of their handicapped child lovingly, always screening her problem from the public. Rosemary grew up with her brothers and sisters, but was never able to keep pace, as lively as they were. In her early 20s, she was placed in a Catholic institution in Wisconsin. Later, in the knowledge of what retardation means to a family, the Kennedy Foundation would contribute millions to this cause.

Jack Kennedy's education began at the Dexter School, a private day school a short walk from his home in Brookline. After moving to Riverdale, New York, he attended Riverdale Country School, again close to home. When the family moved to an 11-bedroom red-brick mansion in Bronxville, he continued at Riverdale School, where he went by bus.

At 13 Jack was sent by his father to the Canterbury School, a Catholic boarding school in New Milford, Connecticut. It was the first time he had been away from home. Jack and his brother Bobby were the only Kennedy boys to attend Catholic school. Their father believed that secular schools would provide a broader outlook; the children received their religious education in their home and church. Rose, however, chose to send their daughters to Catholic school.

Previous pages: *The Kennedy summer home at Hyannis Port, Cape Cod, purchased during the booming 1920s.*

Opposite top: *Jack Kennedy, dressed up as a Keystone cop, is admired by his sister Kathleen.*

Opposite bottom: *The inseparable Kennedy brothers, Joe Jr and Jack, during the first summer at Hyannis Port (1925).*

Above: *The growing Kennedy clan at Hyannis Port in 1925: Rosemary, Jack, Eunice, Joe Jr and Kathleen.*

Right: *Jack, Rosemary, Kathleen and Eunice in 1925, when the seventh of the nine Kennedy children, Robert, was born.*

Left: *The Wallingford, Connecticut, campus of the Choate School (now coeducational Choate Rosemary Hall), where John F Kennedy attended prep school from 1913 until his graduation in 1935. At Choate, Jack Kennedy was hard pressed to match his brother Joe's academic and athletic records.* Below: *Impromptu football games were a perennial feature of life at Hyannis Port: here Jack and Edward practice their passing.*

Jack Kennedy was not an especially good speller in his work at school or in the letters he wrote home, but he did like literature. He wrote to his family that 'We are reading Ivanhoe . . . and the last time we had an exam on it I got ninety-eight.'

It was during the 1931 spring term that he contracted acute appendicitis. He had been losing some weight, but this had been attributed to a lack of milk in his diet. (In 1931 the nutritional importance of vitamins was not yet fully understood, and the parents of a thin child like John Kennedy would have been told to give him three square meals a day and a lot of milk.) His appendix was removed on 2 May 1931 at a hospital in Danbury, Connecticut.

Many years later, when John F Kennedy entered political life, questions and rumors flew as to the state of his health. The need to know if a candidate for public office, particularly the presidency, has the physical fitness to do his job is obvious. Two questions about Kennedy's health were outstanding. One concerned the serious back problem which had plagued him for years. The other was whether or not he had Addison's Disease, a critical adrenal insufficiency, and if so, was it something that might have begun in his youth?

Having spent less than a year at Canterbury School, Jack Kennedy did not return after his appendectomy. He spent the summer recovering at Hyannis Port, being plied with nourishing meals and ice cream by his mother. No record reveals that his health then was different from that of any other youngster recovering from appendicitis. Before he was three years old, he had had all the usual childhood illnesses that are preventible today – scarlet fever, whooping cough, measles, chicken pox. His mother's file cards do not

Right: *An informal graduation picture of Jack Kennedy on the Choate campus in 1935. Although his prep-school performance was uneven, his classmates perceptively voted him 'most likely to succeed.'*
Below: *With classmates, from left, Robert Gibson and Maurice Shea, shortly before their graduation from Choate.*

show unusually severe bouts with these diseases, but she has written that he was frail and sickly as a small child.

That autumn, Kennedy entered the Choate School, a college preparatory school in Wallingford, Connecticut, some 60 miles from his home in Bronxville. His brother Joe was already a student there, two years ahead of him, and popular for his prowess in sports. He was also an academic leader.

The Choate campus was a picture-book version of a New England private school – spacious, tree-shaded, dotted with athletic fields and dormitories. Kennedy was assigned a room next to that of the football coach, who also served as housemaster. This may have been disquieting, given Jack Kennedy's reputation for untidiness, lateness to classes, practical jokes and lack of application to his studies.

In an attempt to equal his brother, Kennedy went out for football immediately, but was never able to become a varsity athlete. He did, however, play on his class team. Encouraged by his father to take part in school sports, he tried a number of them, but could never match his brother's record. Because he lacked weight, it was said, an assistant to his father, Eddie Moore, bribed him to gain some at a dollar a pound. If he was able to get any money this way, it didn't show. He remained wiry and thin.

When Franklin D Roosevelt became President in 1933, Jack Kennedy was 15. His brother Edward had been born the year before. The fall Jack began his second year at Choate, his parents went to Europe with James Roosevelt, the son of the President-to-be. Thinking ahead to the end of Prohibition, Joe Kennedy Sr returned home as agent for three British distillers, Haig & Haig, John Dewar and Gordon's Gin.

Always concerned that his children should excel in their studies, Joseph Kennedy kept after his second

The Kennedys were enthusiastic sailors during their summers at Hyannis Port. Here Jack and Edward maneuver one of the family craft off Cape Cod.

son about his frequently sinking grades. The reply was, 'I hope my marks go up,' but for some time this remained little more than hope.

One wonders how he was able to continue at a school with high academic standards, but somehow he did. What he did have going for him was a gleeful, puckish sense of humor that endeared him to his classmates, but became the bane of his headmaster's existence.

When the family was together, there were always lively dinner-table discussions, 'mostly about personalities, not issues,' Jack Kennedy reportedly said later, adding that he didn't have 'any particular interest in political subjects in those days.'

The spring that Roosevelt became President, Jack Kennedy first met the classmate who was to become one of his closest lifelong friends, LeMoyne Billings. They were both on the staff of the Choate yearbook, *The Brief.* Kennedy was the business manager and Lem, as he was called, the advertising manager. This was one of the activities at which Kennedy was successful. (Another was reported to be a pie-eating contest.)

The month Kennedy entered his third year, or fifth form, at Choate, he had his tonsils and adenoids removed. This was often routinely done at that time, but today it is known that the tonsils act to protect against infection, and they are usually taken out only if they become inflamed. Without any apparent problem from this surgery, he then spent the autumn in school activities much like those of the previous year, continuing as business manager of *The Brief,* trying his best at sports, and being scolded for his grades. To the dismay of his parents, his superior intelligence – to which even his headmaster testified – was not manifesting itself. At Christmas, he and his friend LeMoyne spent their vacation together at the Kennedy winter home in Palm Beach. Later that winter, he experienced what his headmaster, George St John, described in a reference letter to Harvard as a 'severe illness,' unidentified. The letter went on to say that despite his recovery, he 'has not, probably, been able to work under full pressure' due to below par vitality. Nor was he allowed to participate in any 'very vigorous athletics.' One unofficial source described the illness as 'double pneumonia,' but his mother wrote years later that he had had a viral infection that resulted in swollen glands and a bad knee.

With a poor start in the first quarter of his sixth form, Kennedy's last year at Choate, he began trying harder to bring up his grades. He wrote to his father

We're puttin' on our top hat,

Tyin' up our white tie,

Brushin' off our tails,

In order to
Wish you

A Merry Christmas

Opposite: *Jack and life-long friend LeMoyne 'Lem' Billings with 'Dunker' in Europe, 1937, after Kennedy entered Harvard.*
Above: *A group Christmas greeting from Choate days, when Jack Kennedy and his friends were often in trouble. At one point, Joe Kennedy Sr was summoned to the school for a talk.*

that he had 'definitely decided to stop fooling around.' His school work apparently did improve, but Headmaster St John questioned whether his behavior had changed. 'Mucker' was a slang word of the time to describe someone who was against authority, the establishment and the world of adults. Jack Kennedy and his roommate, LeMoyne, organized a secret club, the Muckers. Their symbol was a gold charm, a small shovel. The pranks they carried out under this symbol were described later by the headmaster as 'just peccadilloes.' The Muckers Club, he also wrote, 'had a quality of imagination . . . that few have had.' But meanwhile, St John's time was equally divided between running the school and running Jack Kennedy and his friends.

Short of expelling the group, which had been considered, he called in Joseph Kennedy for a 'three-cornered' conference with his son. The elder Kennedy was then chairman of the Securities and Exchange Commission, appointed by President Roosevelt. What he thought about attending this meeting can only be surmised, but Headmaster St John recalled that he 'spoke very, very strongly' to Jack, 'also with some Irish wit.'

Apparently impressed by this meeting, Kennedy completed his school year uneventfully. Before he left, though, he was voted most likely to succeed by his classmates, whether or not they believed it. He graduated in June 1935, eighteen years old, 64th in a class of 112.

Like his brother Joe before him, Jack Kennedy was sent by their father to study under the socialist economist Harold Laski at the London School of Economics. This may have seemed an unlikely course of study for a Catholic graduate of Choate, but it fulfilled his father's view that education should pre-

pare one to see both sides of an issue. While Joe, Jr, had won praise from Laski for his understanding of economic theory, before the course was well underway, Jack Kennedy became sick with what has been described as hepatitis. Jaundiced and shaken, he was forced to return home.

Joe Kennedy, Sr was a Harvard alumnus and Joe, Jr was a student there. Jack Kennedy was expected to follow their lead, but after his recovery he decided to enroll at Princeton, where his close friends from Choate had gone. Classes had been going on for weeks, but despite his late entry, he made up all of the required studies. By Christmas his illness had recurred in a severe form. This time he was hospitalized for weeks and then sent to an Arizona ranch to recuperate.

While recovering his health that year, 1936, Jack Kennedy made up his mind to enter Harvard as a freshman in the class of 1940, rather than return to Princeton where he would be a year behind his classmates. He had become convinced, for whatever

Below: *When a back injury disqualified him for football, Kennedy tried out for the Harvard swim team in his junior year (second row, third left).*

Opposite top: *This 1937 photograph of Jack Kennedy at 20 captures a sense of the transition from awkward adolescence to emerging maturity.*
Above: *Harvard's Junior Varsity football team in the fall of 1937: Jack Kennedy, in his sophomore year, is in the second row from the top, third from right.*

reason, that he should take his chances with Harvard. His brother Joe, a popular member of the class of 1938, was on the football squad, a class officer, an honor student – everything that the Kennedy sons had been conditioned to seek as goals. Jack Kennedy went out for freshman football, golf and swimming, earning his letters. In his classes – English, French, history and economics – he was an average student. He was chairman of the annual Freshman Smoker, bringing in entertainment – a New York singer with a cast of 40. There was little here to measure against his brother's achievements.

In his sophmore year, Jack Kennedy had to settle for junior varsity, but he played with total determination. Torbert MacDonald, who was later voted to the Harvard Football Hall of Fame and became a Congressman from Massachusetts, was his roommate. Reportedly, he considered his friend a good, well-coordinated athlete, but lacking in the weight and speed to become a top varsity player. It was during a hard scrimmage that year that Kennedy suffered the back injury – a ruptured disc in the lower lumbar area – which plagued him for the rest of his life. He did not play football again at Harvard.

Left: *In Venice with friends, during one of the family's frequent trips to Europe, this one in 1937. A year later, Joseph P Kennedy would be appointed Ambassador to Great Britain's Court of St James.*
Below: *The well-traveled Kennedys ended up in Egypt shortly before World War II broke out in Europe.*

During his junior year, Kennedy tried out for the swimming squad. Competition against Yale was a highly sought position, for which he and Richard Tregaskis, who later wrote *Guadalcanal Diary*, were competing. Then Kennedy caught what must have been a minor virus, and was confined by the doctor to Stillman Infirmary. Unhappy with his hospital food, he had his roommate, 'Torby,' sneak in chocolate milkshakes and cheeseburgers. Later, his friend smuggled him out of the infirmary for practice when no one was at the pool. At his discharge, Kennedy had missed only a few days of practice. The tryouts were held – and Tregaskis won.

At Harvard and afterward, Kennedy had his share of female friends, largely from his own social background. Young women found him attractive and fun, with an outstanding sense of humor. None of these relationships developed into a serious courtship, as marriage was out of the question until he had finished school.

It was during his junior year in college that Kennedy first showed an interest in matters beyond his immediate circle. When his father was appointed Ambassador to Britain's Court of St James in 1938, Jack Kennedy asked Harvard for approval of a plan to spend his spring semester of 1939 overseas, working on a fact-finding tour for his father. The request was granted, and he spent seven months traveling

through a Europe ready to erupt into war, gathering information and writing reports. His spelling was still considered 'atrocious,' but in writing about what he saw in his journey through France, Germany, Poland, Russia, Turkey, Palestine and Egypt, he grew in awareness.

The young Kennedy was in the gallery of Parliament on 3 September 1939, when Prime Minister Neville Chamberlain declared war on Nazi Germany. Americans packed the ships to head home from Europe. The next day Ambassador Kennedy learned that a German submarine had sunk the British liner *Athenia*, an unarmed ship with 300 Americans aboard. The survivors were brought to Glasgow, Scotland. Joe Kennedy sent his eldest son with his friend and aide,

Left: *A family portrait from 1938, when the youngest child, Edward (front row, second from right) was six years old. Jack Kennedy was 14 years old when his brother, nicknamed 'Ted,' was born. Below: Taken at the old Midway Airport in Chicago during Kennedy's last year at Harvard – 1940. After a lackluster performance at prep school, Kennedy redeemed himself at college, where his native intelligence manifested itself more and more with increasing maturity.*

Eddie Moore, to care for the Americans rescued. Seventeen days later, Jack Kennedy came home, having seen first-hand the effects of war, and ready to start his senior year at Harvard.

From these experiences came Kennedy's idea for his thesis, *Appeasement at Munich: The Inevitable Result of the Slowness of the British Democracy to a Change from a Disarmament Policy.* His senior paper enabled him to graduate with honors in political science. Edited and retitled *Why England Slept*, it was published with the help of Arthur Krock, a friend of his father, with a foreword by publisher Henry Luce. An instant best-seller, the book sold 80,000 copies in the United States and England. Certainly Jack Kennedy had been deeply influenced by his father's view of the European crisis and helped in many ways to get the book published, but he worked on his thesis and book with more energy than he had brought to any previous study. In the process, his mind opened to political and public issues. He graduated from Harvard *cum laude* in 1940.

In 23 years Jack Kennedy had come a long way from the days of 'political lullabies' in Brookline. A Harvard degree in political science and a book on British disarmament policy were indicative of the fact that he was working toward his own views of the world and his place in it. The opportunity to travel abroad, and to study history as it unfolded, was undoubtedly a factor in turning his attention to a wider sphere. His abilities had been tested by the time his country entered World War II.

'In Keeping with the Highest Traditions...'

With a war going on in Europe, and the uncertainty this created in the United States, planning for a civilian life after college was difficult for Jack Kennedy, as it was for many young men in 1940. In his Harvard yearbook, he had listed his intended vocation as law. There had also been talk of journalism as a career, or something in education, or perhaps even business, following in the footsteps of his father. Joe Jr was already attending Harvard Law School. Jack Kennedy thought of entering Yale Law School, which would be similar to the path his brother had taken. However, when September came, he enrolled instead in the graduate business school of Stanford University to audit some courses in business administration and political science.

In *Why England Slept*, Kennedy had written: 'To say that democracy has been awakened . . . is not enough. What we need is an armed guard that will wake up when the fire starts or, better yet, one that will not permit a fire to start at all.' The Kennedys, father and sons, were against intervention in foreign wars, but they believed strongly in a prepared America. Ambassador Kennedy had been drawing criticism, in both England and the United States, of his position,

Opposite: *Rose, Jack and Eunice Kennedy at Sugarloaf Mountain, Rio de Janeiro, during the 1941 trip to Latin America.*

Above: *Joseph P Kennedy, seen here at a press conference with Jack at his right, antagonized President Roosevelt by his opposition to US entry into World War II.*

which appeared to be one of appeasement and isolationism. His relationship with President Roosevelt had deteriorated: there were rumors that he might oppose Roosevelt's election to a third term. But in the fall, when Ambassador Kennedy came home from England, the president sought a renewal of his support. Convinced finally that Roosevelt would keep the United States out of war, Kennedy made a radio address on behalf of President Roosevelt in which he said: 'My wife and I have given nine hostages to fortune. Our children and your children are more important than anything else in the world. The kind of America that they and their children inherit is of grave concern to us all.' On that same day, 29 October, a national lottery was held in Washington, DC. Secretary of War Henry L Stimson reached into a jar holding 9000 serial numbers of draft registrants. *The New York Times* reported later that 'John Kennedy, one

Honolulu Star-Bulletin 1st EXTR

8 PAGES—HONOLULU, TERRITORY OF HAWAII, U. S. A., SUNDAY, DECEMBER 7, 1941—8 PAGES

★ PRICE FI

WAR!

OAHU BOMBED BY JAPANESE PLANES

(Associated Press by Transpacific Telephone)

SAN FRANCISCO, Dec. 7.—P
ident Roosevelt announced
morning that Japanese planes
attacked Manila and Pearl Har

Left: *The news of the Japanese attack on Pearl Harbor stuns the nation: 7 December 1941. John F Kennedy had already applied for a commission in the US Navy, only four months before.*
Below: *An aerial view of Pearl Harbor, anchorage of the US Pacific Fleet, taken only weeks before the bombing.*

of the nine, had become No. 18 on Palo Alto, California, draft board rolls. Mr Kennedy, whose serial number is 2748, is a graduate student at Stanford University.'

Jack Kennedy supported the draft on the Stanford campus, but his father resigned his ambassadorial post not long after Roosevelt's re-election. While at Stanford, Kennedy served as a reporter at an Institute of World Affairs conference in Riverside, California, writing summary reports of the sessions. By now he had a highly developed interest in politics, and was considered by everyone who knew him to be very well read and informed. He was also enjoying the California sun and the social life, and rooting for one of Stanford's finest football teams. But in December, after spending Christmas with his family, he required medical treatment in Boston's Lahey Clinic and the New England Baptist Hospital. While hospitalized, he contributed an article, published 2 February 1941, to the New York *Journal American* headlined 'Irish Bases Vital to Britain.'

It has been reported that Jack Kennedy was able to pass a physical for military service after spending five months conditioning his weak back with special exercises. These exercises may well have been prescribed for him during this period of medical treatment in Boston. In the past, many patients with disc problems that caused extreme sciatica, or nerve pain, which is what John Kennedy was said to have, had a form of major low-back surgery called a laminectomy. But conservative measures called for bed rest, medication and exercise. Any other health problems that may

Left: *A Japanese Aichi D3A Val dive bomber noses over onto its target with its underwing dive brakes deployed.*
Below: *USS Pennsylvania was one of eight battleships sunk at their moorings, yet all but two were later raised and repaired.*

have existed, whether an infection like hepatitis, or, as has been suggested, an adrenal insufficiency, would naturally complicate the medical picture.

In the spring of 1941, Rose and Eunice Kennedy were planning a tour of Latin America. Apparently recovered by May, Jack Kennedy joined them in Rio de Janeiro, then went on alone for a longer tour of South America. On the first of July, he returned to the United States to await the July draft call. A few weeks later, on 24 July 1941, his brother Joe enlisted in the

United States Naval Reserve at the Squantum Naval Air Station near Boston.

Jack Kennedy applied for a commission in the Navy in early August and was sworn in as an ensign in the Naval Reserve on 25 September 1941. Ensign J F Kennedy's first naval assignment was with the Office of Naval Intelligence in Washington, DC. His duty there was with the Foreign Intelligence Branch, a small unit which prepared daily and weekly summaries of principal developments. He was part of this group when Pearl Harbor was attacked on 7 December 1941.

According to published reports, Kennedy was dating at this time a young woman who was a friend of his sister Kathleen. Inga Arvad was a Danish journalist working in Washington for Cissie Patterson's newspaper, the *Times-Herald*. President Roosevelt was not friendly to the *Times-Herald*. Harold L Ickes, then Secretary of the Interior, explained why in his book *The Lowering Clouds:* 'Last Thursday the *Chicago Tribune*, the *New York Daily News* and the *Washington Times-Herald* printed what purported to be secret war plans of the War Department to send an expeditionary force to Europe. It reproduced a letter over the President's signature asking that such plans be made.' He went on to say, 'If we had been at war, this publication would have constituted treason.'

Above: *Joe Kennedy Jr after his enlistment in the US Naval Reserve.*
Right: *Robert F Kennedy joins his brothers in the service (1943), as his father looks on.*
Opposite top: *Ensign Kennedy at Sixth Naval District Headquarters in Charleston, South Carolina, early in 1942. During his brief stint here, Kennedy instructed defense plant workers in anti-bomb measures.*

At some point in his friendship with Inga Arvad, Kennedy apparently learned that she was under surveillance by the FBI. Apparently, she not only had close relationships with others who were under suspicion at the time, but in Europe she had been friendly with Herman Goering. The possibility, however, that she might have been a secret agent was never proved. The fact that she knew Jack came to the attention of the authorities when, 10 days before Pearl Harbor was bombed, she published an article about him in the *Times-Herald*. Later, the American failure to pinpoint where the Japanese would attack created deep anxiety in the Office of Naval Intelligence. The resulting shakeup affected Ensign Kennedy, who was transferred to the Sixth Naval District Headquarters at Charleston, South Carolina. His job was that of instructing defense plant workers in methods of protection from bombs.

After working in Charleston for several months on a job he found frustrating, Kennedy asked for a transfer to the Fourteenth Naval District in Honolulu, Hawaii. Although the assignment would be in Intelligence, and not on sea duty, the area was closer to the action. Kennedy had an intense desire to be on the front lines, to see combat, as did so many young men of the time. His need to be where the action was in any situation caused him as much pain as his back problem, which he may well have known was keeping him from active duty. While waiting for an answer to his request for transfer, he went to Boston for a consultation with his private physicians. He then asked the Navy for six months' inactive duty to undergo the operation recommended (unnamed in public records, but probably a laminectomy) plus a period of convalescence. To get out on the front lines, he was willing to risk any adverse results of the surgery. Also, he explained to his Navy superiors, the operation would be paid for out of Kennedy funds.

The Navy first sent Kennedy to the Charleston Naval Hospital for a confirmation of his condition. He was then transferred to the Chelsea Naval Hospital at Boston, where he received treatment, but apparently no surgery was performed. This treatment may have been considered successful by the Navy, or perhaps Joseph Kennedy sought the help of a friend for his action-minded son. In any event, on 27 July 1942, Jack Kennedy finally reported to Northwestern University in Chicago for the officer training course, a preparation for sea duty.

A publicity campaign to recruit men for PT boat service was underway while Kennedy was training at Northwestern. Medal of Honor winner John D Bulkeley, the PT boat commander who had brought General Douglas MacArthur and his family to safety before the Philippine Islands fell, was one of the recruiters. John Harllee, who was executive officer and senior instructor at the Motor Torpedo Boat Training Center at Melville, Rhode Island, was an-

Above: *Kennedy made lasting friends during his US Navy service, including, from left, George Ross, Leonard J Thom, Paul B 'Red' Fay Jr and James Reed, seen here relaxing at Hyannis Port with their host and Bernard Lyons (1944).*
Left: *Ensign Kennedy in the Solomon Islands, on the sea duty that had been denied him during his first year in the navy. He served nine months in the South Pacific, and emerged as a war hero for his role in the rescue of the men under his command in PT 109, destroyed in combat on 2 August 1943.*
Right: *The Motor Torpedo Boat Training Center at Melville, Rhode Island, where Kennedy (back row, seventh from end) was stationed with his friend Torbert MacDonald. They had hoped to be assigned to the same squadron in the combat zone, but Kennedy was kept on at Melville as an instructor, to his disappointment.*

other. With Kennedy's boating experience, personality and education, and obviously strong desire to get into action, he had no trouble being selected.

On 1 October 1942, Kennedy was at the PT boat training school in Melville. Planning and help from Ambassador Kennedy enabled him and his former Harvard roommate, Torbert MacDonald, to be stationed together there. Part of their plan was eventual assignment to the same squadron, but this was not to be. At Melville, Kennedy met someone who would also become a lifelong friend and eventually Undersecretary of the Navy for the New Frontier. This was Ensign Paul B 'Red' Fay Jr, who in 1966 would publish his memories of the former president in the book *The Pleasure of His Company*.

Kennedy and MacDonald finished at the Motor Torpedo Boat Training Center at about the same time in December 1942. But MacDonald, to their dismay, was assigned to a PT boat in the combat zone, while Kennedy was kept on at Melville as an instructor. It was at this time that he got the nickname 'Shafty': Torby MacDonald claimed that his friend had been 'shafted' by the Navy.

JFKennedy

Now a Lieutenant (jg), J F Kennedy took command of his first boat, PT 101, at Melville on 7 December 1942, exactly one year after the Japanese attack on Pearl Harbor. A few weeks later, he was transferred with PT 101 to Squadron Fourteen at Jacksonville, Florida, which was scheduled for extended duty in the Panama Canal Zone. When Kennedy learned that he would have to remain in Panama, he was extremely unhappy, but his father interceded for him again. With the help of Massachusetts Senator David I Walsh, who was then Chairman of the Senate Naval Affairs Committee, and Secretary of the Navy James Forrestal, another Kennedy friend, he was reassigned. By 10 March 1943, Lt J F Kennedy was on his way from San Diego to the South Pacific aboard the converted French liner *Rochambeau*. Her destination was Espiritu Santo in the New Hebrides, a thousand miles northeast of Australia. From there he would go on to his new post at Tulagi, in the Solomon Islands.

At Espiritu Santo, Kennedy was transferred to LST 449, which carried men and ammunition to the Guadalcanal and Tulagi area. On the third day out, as LST 449 was approaching Guadalcanal, the transport was warned that a Japanese air raid was imminent.

Main picture: *Navy transports at anchor off Guadalcanal, Solomon Islands, during the Pacific campaign.*
Inset: *US transports leave Tulagi during the Solomons campaign, in a view taken from USS* Chicago. *Even after the US capture of the Japanese airfield on Guadalcanal (1942), the Solomon Islands were hotly contested because of their proximity to Australia and their strategic role in the US counteroffensive against Japan.*
Below: *Lieutenant Kennedy flanked by George Ross, at left, Red Fay (who would be Undersecretary of the Navy in the Kennedy Administration) and James Reed at Tulagi.*

Told to retreat, LST 449 headed back toward Espiritu Santo, joined by the destroyer *Aaron Ward* and subchaser 521 as an escort. Several hours later, Japanese bombers located the small convoy and began their assault. Using evasive tactics, LST 449 escaped without serious damage, but the engine room of *Aaron Ward* took a direct hit. An attempt was made to tow her, but a few miles short of her objective, Tulagi, she sank.

Sometime during the battle, a Japanese plane was downed, leaving a life-belted pilot alive in the water. The LST 449 made a pass to retrieve him, with crew members and passengers watching at the rail. But at their approach, the Japanese flier shot at them several times, until he was killed by gunfire from the transport.

After cruising in the area for almost a week, LST 449 arrived at Tulagi on 14 April 1943. Jack Kennedy had been introduced to war in the South Pacific. Some ten days later, 25 April, at 1100 hours, Lt Kennedy assumed command of PT 109, which had already seen heavy combat. Her engines were faulty due to bad fuel, and she needed refurbishing.

Officially, a PT boat required 12 men, but at Tulagi, a few less was the norm. When Kennedy signed on, his crew was all of two men: Ensign Leonard J Thom, the executive officer, and another man who was soon replaced. With a crew changeover in progress, the first task was to pick new men from the arriving replacements. A week and a half later there were six more men in the group; by the end of May, one man had been replaced and another had joined them.

While the crew was forming, PT 109 was overhauled. On 29 April a series of nighttime training patrols began. With an undermanned boat, it was vital that everyone be able to take on any job. In fact, there was little else going on: it was a time of preparation for the planned invasion of New Georgia.

Jack Kennedy was 26 years old on 29 May. The next day he and his men left Tulagi for Russell Island, closer to the planned invasion area. Their new base was primitive, the weather was miserably hot, and the men looked jaundiced from regular doses of atabrine, the antimalarial drug. The night patrols continued, still essentially as training, but also to secure the area against possible undetected forces.

In mid-July, Kennedy and his crew were ordered to advance to the front-line base at Lumbari Island, off northeast Rendova. Some 25 torpedo boats were at the Lumbari base under the command of Thomas Glover Warfield.

The Japanese, intent on reinforcing their garrisons on New Georgia and Kolobangara, ran frequent night convoys – the Tokyo Express. Japanese barges moved supplies and men between garrisons, protected by large guns and heavy armor plate. The duty of the

Opposite: *The light cruiser US St Louis leaves Tulagi Harbor in 1943, when Kennedy participated in the US Navy effort to clear the Solomons (the Japanese still had garrisons on New Georgia and Kolobangara at this time).*
Right: *The crew of PT 109, which was slightly undermanned – the normal complement for a PT boat was 12 men, not 10. Their main job was to interdict resupply of the Japanese garrisons on New Georgia and Kolobangara, carried out mainly by night convoys nicknamed the Tokyo Express.*
Below: *At the helm of PT 109: Kennedy's experience and skill with small boats made him a natural candidate for this command.*

Above: *US Navy night-fighting techniques improved during the long fight for Guadalcanal in 1942, but Japanese night-supply operations remained a problem throughout*

Kennedy's 1943 tour of duty in the Solomons.
Opposite: *Convalescing from back surgery, Kennedy receives the Navy and Marine Corps Medal from hospital commandant Captain Conklin.*

plywood-hulled PT boats was to search out and destroy, to blockade, to give warning of any Japanese traffic. The Japanese countered by dropping flares and bombs.

PT 109 performed these missions unharmed until the night of 19 July, when a party went out to confront an expected convoy that it failed to locate. As the Americans were about to give up, a Japanese plane discovered them. PT 109 was directly in the light of a flare. Kennedy began evasive tactics, but several bombs hit close to the boat, wounding two crew members with shrapnel. These men had to be replaced on return to Lumbari, where two additional members also joined the crew. However, the new members were comparatively untried in combat, which would make a difference in the following weeks. Another man was in a state of shock from the bombing.

There are many and contradictory stories about what happened to PT 109 and her crew in the early morning hours of 2 August 1943, and during the following week. *The New York Times* printed this one:

KENNEDY'S SON IS HERO IN PACIFIC
AS DESTROYER SPLITS HIS PT BOAT
A UNITED STATES TORPEDO BASE, New Georgia, Aug. 8 (Delayed) – Out of the darkness, a Japanese destroyer appeared suddenly. It sliced diagonally in two the PT boat skippered by Lieut. (j.g.) John F. Kennedy, son of the former Ambassador in London, Joseph P. Kennedy.

Crews of two other PT boats, patrolling close by, saw flaming high octane gasoline spread over the water. They gave up "Skipper" Kennedy and all his crew as lost the morning of Aug. 2.

But Lieutenant Kennedy, 26, and ten of his men were rescued today from a small coral island deep inside Japanese-controlled Solomon Islands territory, and within range of enemy shore guns.

On 2 August 15 PT boats had been ordered out to meet the expected Japanese convoy: 109 was in Division B, consisting of three boats. The battle of Blackett Strait became a scene of confused commands and actions, and the circumstances surrounding the ram-

ming of PT 109 are unknown. By his own account, Jack Kennedy's thought when it occurred was: 'This is how it feels to be killed.'

Two men were lost immediately; several others were severely injured and burned. Kennedy had been slammed against a frame of the cockpit, but was still conscious. Fearing the floating hulk would explode, the crew went overboard, to be swept away in the water, which was covered by burning gas. Choking on the fumes, they struggled to return to the bow section when it was seen that this would offer some security. Kennedy tried to keep his men together and to rescue the badly burned Machinist's Mate, Patrick McMahon.

The men drifted for hours, clinging to the hulk. When it seemed their refuge was going to sink, they decided to try for an island three and a half miles away (closer islands were held by the Japanese). Kennedy towed McMahon, who was too badly burned to swim. When their island position was secured, he left the men with his executive officer, Leonard Thom, and went to look for a means of rescue. He swam out several miles to Ferguson Passage, where the PT boats usually patrolled, with a heavy battle lantern. There he swam and treaded water in a fruitless search for help that ended in exhaustion. He washed up on a tiny island called Leorava.

Late that morning Kennedy was able to return to his crew, but he collapsed again with exhaustion. By 4 August hunger and thirst impelled the marooned men toward a larger island, Olasana. They swam there in three hours, clinging to debris and towing the injured McMahon, but the island offered no better food than green coconuts, which made them sick. They still lacked fresh water.

Meanwhile, Navy aircraft sent out to look for survivors had failed to spot them, but an intelligence operative for the Australian Navy, Lt Arthur R Evans, had a secret outpost inside Japanese territory. High on the side of a mountain on the island of Kolobangara, it overlooked Blackett Strait where the battle had taken place. With the help of a network of friendly natives, Evans was gathering information on the passage of Japanese ships and activities on the Japanese bases. In the process, he had seen the explosion of PT 109 and later its floating hulk, but had not observed any survivors. His radio report to the US Navy led to an alert to local natives, which resulted in the eventual discovery of the missing men.

Kennedy and Ensign George Ross, who was not a member of the crew, but who had unluckily come along on the ill-fated mission, decided to explore nearby Naru Island for food and water. There they found a native dugout canoe, a drum of water and

Right: *When he became president, Kennedy kept the coconut on which he had carved his message to the base at Rendova on his desk in the Oval Office. His military record was a major asset when he campaigned for election io the House of Representatives from Boston's 11th District. As his friend David F Powers recalled it later, 'We never had an election like 1946 – if you didn't have the word* veteran *beside your name, you couldn't be elected dog-catcher.'*

Left: *With LeMoyne Billings, his friend since prep-school days, at Palm Beach, after Kennedy had been assigned to stateside duty in Miami on account of his recurring back problem (1944).*

Lt Joseph P Kennedy Jr, seen here with his father, served with distinction as a US Navy pilot until 12 August 1944, when he was killed in action over the English Channel.

some crackers and hard candy. At that point, two native scouts for Lt Evans were seen at a distance by Kennedy and Ross. Neither party made contact, for fear the other was Japanese. The natives then canoed to Olasana Island, where the rest of the crew enticed the scouts ashore and convinced them that they were, indeed, Americans. Uncertain of the whereabouts of Kennedy and Ross, Ensign Thom wrote a note for the natives to take to the base at Rendova.

Meanwhile, Kennedy had piled the food and water found on Naru Island into the dugout canoe and was returning to Olasana. When he learned of the situation there, the rescue of all the men seemed reasonably assured. Apparently to prevent any possible mixup in messages, Kennedy carved his later-to-be-famous note on a coconut with his sheath knife:

NATIVE KNOWS POSIT
HE CAN PILOT 11 ALIVE NEED
SMALL BOAT
KENNEDY

Ensign Ross had been badly cut on the coral reef and needed medical care. The scouts made contact with Lt Evans, who managed the rescue arrangements with

the Rendova base. Two war correspondents, learning of the planned rescue of the 109 crew and the son of a former ambassador, went along on the secret mission through enemy territory. By the time Kennedy and his men were back at Rendova, getting medical attention, the correspondents had their story.

Kennedy was determined to stay at the Lumbari PT boat base, although he was eligible for leave. The idea of converting some of the PT boats into gunboats was now being considered seriously. The plan was to remove the torpedoes, add heavier guns and provide armor plate for the plywood hull. Kennedy volunteered for the job of seeing the plan through. When this was accomplished, he was given command of the first converted vessel, PT 59, after promotion to full Lieutenant. Among his crew were five members of his former command.

The war began to move away from the area around New Georgia during the next few months. The Japanese were disbanding their garrisons, and the PT Boat patrols gradually diminished. Kennedy's newly converted PT 59 was sent to a forward base, Lambu Lambu, to take up patrolling closer to Bougainville.

The last major action in which Lt Kennedy participated was the rescue of 80 Marines who had become surrounded during the battle of Bougainville on the first two days of November. The rescued Marines were brought out of the area on LCPLs – Landing Craft, Personnel, Large – but one of the craft was damaged and sinking. PT 59 took on board 10 Marines, three of whom were seriously wounded. Before they reached the safety of Lambu Lambu, one of the injured men died in Kennedy's bunk. That night, PT 59 returned to help evacuate the main Marine base.

Two weeks later the logbook of PT 59 recorded: '1430: Lt. Kennedy left the boat as directed by the Dr. at Lambu Lambu.' Kennedy was suffering from his chronic disc problem and could no longer deny it. He returned to the United States shortly after Christmas, having spent nine months in the South Pacific. Until 27 May 1944, he was stationed in Miami, Florida, where the Navy had a PT boat shakedown unit. He was then transferred to the Boston area, first to the Chelsea Naval Hospital, and then to the New England Baptist Hospital for a disc operation. Before the operation, Kennedy was photographed receiving a medal. He looked thin and unwell. *The New York Times* reported under date line Washington, 11 June that 'The Navy and Marine Corps Medal has been awarded to Lieut. John F. Kennedy, son of Joseph P.

Kennedy, former United States Ambassador to Great Britain, for "extremely heroic conduct" when his PT boat was cut in two and sunk by a destroyer.' The official citation ended: 'His outstanding courage, endurance and leadership contributed to the saving of several lives and were in keeping with the highest traditions of the United States Naval Service.'

After surgery, Kennedy spent the next three months recuperating at the New England Baptist Hospital. He was preparing for release to physical therapy at the Chelsea Naval Hospital when he learned that his brother Joe had been killed in action. On 12 August 1944, Lt Joseph P Kennedy, Jr had been shot down while piloting a B-24 carrying 22,000 pounds of explosives across the English Channel to a V-2 rocket site in Normandy.

Below: *US Marines awaiting evacuation of their main base on Bougainville by LCPLs and PT boats, including Kennedy's (1-3 November 1943). Two weeks later, Kennedy left the Solomon Islands for the United States.*

Above: *US Marines in the Battle of Bougainville, November 1943. This was the last major action in which Kennedy – who had been promoted to full lieutenant – participated. As the skipper of PT 59, with five crewmen from his former command and several others, he helped rescue 80 US Marines who had been surrounded on the island.*

'To Serve My Country in Peace...'

Senator Kennedy in his Washington office after the prolonged illness during which he wrote Profiles in Courage.

When Jack's brother Joe was killed, the Kennedy family lost not only their much-loved oldest son, but his father's hope of getting his namesake into politics – perhaps all the way to the White House. There was speculation for years, none of it denied by Jack Kennedy himself, that this determined, ambitious father then tapped his second son to take his brother's place.

John F Kennedy was not a natural politician of the old school – a hearty backslapper setting strategy in a smoke-filled back room. Reserved rather than shy, he had the kind of personality that was attractive without

being familiar. And whatever he did, he related his experience to his intense, idealistic interest in politics. Jack was not just a carbon copy of his older brother. He too had grown up on politics, but he had to learn to be a politician.

While still at Chelsea Naval Hospital during the fall of 1944, Jack put together a collection of tributes to his dead brother, intending it as a Christmas present for his parents. This was printed later in the memorial volume *As We Remember Joe*. Then, finally able to walk again, on 16 March 1945, Lt John F Kennedy received a medical discharge from the United States Navy. For Jack and his brother, fighting the war was over.

To regain his health, Jack went out to the Arizona ranch where he had gone after he dropped out of Princeton. He was there in April when President Roosevelt died and Harry Truman took over. By the end of that month, now strong enough to work at a civilian job, Kennedy went to San Francisco to cover the founding of the United Nations as a special correspondent for the Hearst newspapers. Germany surrendered on 8 May while the conference was going on. It was VE Day – Victory in Europe. But Jack reported from San Francisco that Americans on the West Coast were deeply concerned about victory over Japan. Their proximity to the Eastern adversary made them more conscious of the war in the Pacific.

British elections were coming up in July, and Kennedy went to England, again as a special correspondent. He believed that Winston Churchill and the Conservatives would win, but instead, the Labourites gained a landslide victory. Winston Churchill lost to Clement Attlee. Kennedy wrote in explanation: 'First, the general feeling that after ten years of Conservative government, it was "time for a change." That was a good slogan of Gov. Dewey when he ran for President against the late President Roosevelt. He was just in the wrong country.'

The Big Three Conference was going on in Potsdam, Germany, at the end of July. Truman and Stalin were there, and Churchill was to be replaced by Attlee. As the son of a former ambassador, Jack was asked to carry a diplomatic pouch to Secretary of State James M Byrnes, who was at the meeting. On Jack's return to London, he became quite sick with what was reportedly diagnosed by Navy doctors as a recurrence of malaria, apparently contracted while he was in the South Pacific. Unable to continue working as a reporter, Kennedy went back to the United States.

While he struggled to regain his health, the war in the Pacific ended. The United States dropped the first

Below: *The War Room in SHAEF headquarters, Reims, where Gustaf Jodl, German Chief of Staff (center, back to camera), signed the German surrender ending hostilities in Europe, which would soon be succeeded by the cold war.*

Above: *On 7 May 1945, General Dwight D Eisenhower, center, and representatives of the Allied Expeditionary Forces accept Germany's unconditional surrender at Reims, France – V-E Day.*
Opposite: *Addressing a GE rally in November 1946, just before his election to Congress as a representative from Boston's 11th District. Kennedy's reputation as a war hero contributed heavily to his victory.*

Left: *British Prime Minister Winston Churchill, right, greeting members of his government. Ambassador Joseph P Kennedy came into conflict with both Churchill and President Roosevelt when he opposed US involvement in World War II. Jack Kennedy had addressed British disarmament policy and its results in his book* Why England Slept.

atomic bomb on Hiroshima, Japan, on 6 August 1945. Three days later, a second atomic bomb struck Nagasaki. Representatives of Imperial Japan signed the formal surrender aboard the USS *Missouri* in Tokyo Bay on 2 September 1945.

Before the war ended, Joseph P Kennedy had put together an elaborate, well-organized machine designed to launch his son into politics. The senior Kennedy accepted an assignment from Massachusetts Governor Maurice Tobin to do an economic survey of the state. This gave him a base from which to become well acquainted with all the people who could be helpful to his son.

Although some would call John F Kennedy a carpetbagger – it had been years since he made his home in Boston – it was natural for him to look to the Eleventh Congressional District of Massachusetts as his political springboard. His roots were there, where his grandparents lived and he and his parents had been born. To establish residency in Boston, Kennedy first took a room at the Bellevue Hotel, a hangout for city politicians. Not long afterward, he got a tiny apartment at 122 Bowdoin Street that would remain his voting residence from then on. An organization of

political pros and amateurs grew up around him. Important as an advisor was his father's cousin Joseph L Kane, who was 66 years old. As Rose Kennedy reflected later, 'Cousin Joe could tell him about the winds and tides, the shoals and channels in this particular form of navigation.'

As much as Jack Kennedy may have welcomed the advice of older politicians, he was determined to speak for the younger generation as well. He enlisted a group composed mainly of young veterans whom he called his 'Little Brain Trust' – to help and advise him. One of these men, David Powers, was to become a trusted friend and aide for life. Powers had intended to work for another politician and was at first unwilling to commit himself, but he agreed to come to a meeting at which Kennedy was speaking. The meeting was of an organization called Gold Star Mothers – women who had lost at least one son in the war. Kennedy's prepared talk ended awkwardly but when he went on to identify with the women by saying that his mother, too, was a Gold Star mother, he won over his audience. Powers was sufficiently impressed to join the Kennedy team: never, he recalled later, had he seen a comparable reaction.

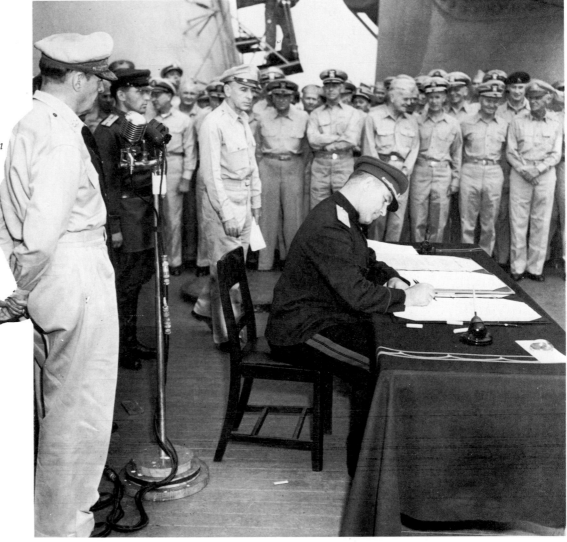

Opposite: *At the Yalta Conference of 4-11 February 1945, Churchill, Roosevelt and Josef Stalin agreed to form the United Nations in San Francisco on 25 April, which John F Kennedy would cover as a special correspondent for the Hearst newspapers.*
Right: *The Japanese surrender, signed aboard the USS* Missouri *in Tokyo Bay, with General Douglas MacArthur (left) accepting the surrender on behalf of the Allies (September 1945). Five months earlier, Harry S Truman had succeeded Roosevelt as president. Fledgling Congressman Jack Kennedy would support Truman.*
Bottom right: *Labourite British Prime Minister Clement Attlee.*

When the buildup for Kennedy's political life began, the office for which he would run had not been decided upon. It was necessary to put him on the public scene first. An ad agency, John C Dowd, Inc, was brought in; later, there would be others. Step by step, the Kennedy name would be kept before the public. The story of PT 109. The story of Joe Kennedy Jr's death. The story of the destroyer USS *Joseph P Kennedy Jr*, commissioned in the Navy yard in the Eleventh Congressional District. On the second anniversary of his brother's death, a memorial foundation was established, with Jack Kennedy as its president. Its first gift was of $600,000 to Archbishop Richard J Cushing for the construction of a children's hospital – also in the Eleventh Congressional District. Jack Kennedy was an idealist, but he was also a realist. He understood the lessons of Cousin Joe Kane, who was reported to have said that politics, like war, takes three things – money, money and more money.

When the former mayor of Boston, James M Curley, decided to run for mayor again, it meant that if he won, he would have to vacate his Congressional seat from the Eleventh District. Curley was an implacable foe of Jack's grandfather, Honey Fitz, and the

Kennedys were ready. In November 1945, Curley became Boston's mayor for the fourth time, leaving the House seat open. Nomination petitions began circulating for Jack Kennedy on 9 April 1946. Two weeks later, he announced his candidacy.

Thin and awkward, looking almost like a high-school debater, Kennedy took up a round of speaking engagements. Although he was obviously sincere in his addresses to Rotary Clubs and American Legion Posts, his ability as a speaker was far removed from the eloquence he would develop with practice. He talked about the war, his war record and the problems of veterans, including their lack of housing, which became an important issue.

Aside from his family's reputation, Jack Kennedy was a virtual unknown in Boston politics. He had to make use of his war record. He was elected chairman of the Veterans of Foreign Wars national convention, which would be held in Boston during September 1946. The Joseph P Kennedy Jr VFW Post was organized, with Jack as commander. Edward F McLaughlin Jr, a friend Jack had made in the Solomon Islands, was named vice-commander.

Opposite top: *A Memorial Day appearance in Cambridge, Massachusetts, on the 1946 campaign trail.*
Opposite bottom: *Jean Kennedy Smith and her parents at the launching of the destroyer USS* Joseph P Kennedy Jr *in the Boston Navy yard.*
Above: *Joseph P Kennedy Sr is greeted by officers and men of the destroyer named for his son – 1946.*
Right: *A fund-raising dinner for Boston's Halsan Orphanage during the 1946 Congressional campaign: speaking with Kennedy is Archbishop (later Cardinal) Richard J Cushing, a close personal friend of the Kennedys, who officiated at family weddings, baptisms and funerals.*

Left: *Kennedy was never comfortable with the kind of ward politics that relied heavily on back-slapping and hearty humor. His natural reserve made it difficult for him to play a credible part in fraternal gatherings like this Knights of Columbus meeting in Boston's Bunker Hill area (1946).*

Bottom left: *The aspiring Congressman casts his vote in Boston's Democratic primaries of June 1946, flanked by his maternal grandparents, Mr and Mrs John F Fitzgerald. His grandfather's status as a former Congressman and Mayor of Boston contributed to Kennedy's success in seeking the same 11th-District seat.*

Left: *Despite his inexperience, Kennedy surprised even his supporters by the magnitude of his victory in the June 1946 primaries for the Congressional seat vacated by former Major of Boston James M Curley, then seeking re-election to the mayoralty. This successful all-out campaign set the tone for those that would follow.*

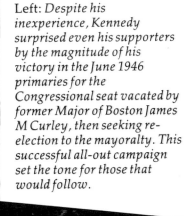

The November 1946 election in Democratic Massachusetts was regarded as an obligatory ritual that allowed a Republican candidate (Lester W Bowen) to participate. The primary, in which Kennedy would face nine other candidates, was the important day. The Kennedy entourage knew that if their man could win the primary, the House seat was his.

The campaign, a masterpiece of strategy, set the standard for all those that would follow. It was particularly notable because it had to be conducted so fast. Primaries, usually held in September, were to take place on 18 June 1946, to give those in military service time to mail in absentee ballots. Last-minute events were turned into triumphs. The largest formal reception Cambridge had ever seen was held for some 1500 women voters on 15 June. Rose Kennedy served as hostess, as she had done for her father, Honey Fitz, when he was mayor of Boston. One hundred thousand reprints of a *Reader's Digest* article on PT 109 were delivered to voters just before the primary. Bunker Hill Day, an important Boston holiday on 17 June, was used to parade members of Jack's VFW Post through town. As the parade ended, he collapsed, sick and in pain. But after the votes were counted, he knew that all the effort had been worthwhile. He received almost double the number of votes obtained by his closest rival. And the November election was, as expected, only a formality.

As a fledgling Congressman, Kennedy explained in

his first speech (January 1947), 'When ships were sinking and young Americans were dying . . . I firmly resolved to serve my country in peace as I honestly tried to serve it in war.'

Eunice Kennedy had volunteered to work as executive secretary for the National Conference on Juvenile Delinquency, a Justice Department committee in Washington. She and her brother decided to rent a house together in Georgetown, where Eunice could serve as his hostess. Here many of their friends, old

and new, would gather, among them another freshman Congressman, Richard M Nixon, who was also a Navy veteran of the Solomons.

The Republican-controlled Eightieth Congress would be in constant conflict with Democratic President Harry S Truman. Beginning public life in this context represented an uphill fight for J F Kennedy. At the outset he received two committee assignments. One was to the District of Columbia Committee, which functioned as the government of the District of

Columbia. The other, considered an unusual assignment for a freshman representative, was to serve on the House Committee on Education and Labor; its chairman was Fred A Hartley Jr of New Jersey. Jack was also asked to serve on a special subcommittee on veterans' housing, an offshoot of the House Veterans' Affairs Committee, chaired by Edith Nourse Rogers of Massachusetts.

Congressman Kennedy's political philosophy and voting record became difficult for many to classify.

His record was described as everything from 'undistinguished' to 'outstanding.' He was not a militant liberal, but neither was he a strict conservative. His roots were in the Democratic Party of Irish-Catholic Boston, which supported the New Deal of Roosevelt and the Fair Deal of Truman.

Kennedy fought vigorously for the Taft-Ellender-Wagner Housing Bill, which was intended to provide Federal money for slum clearance and construction of housing units. On 10 March 1947, he spoke at a

Left: *During his first term in Congress, Kennedy was a strong advocate for veterans' housing, which became an important issue soon after World War II. He also espoused the cause of slum* *clearance and renovation.*
Above: *A visit to the Boston docks during 1952, when Kennedy sought the Senate seat that had been held by Henry Cabot Lodge since 1936.*

National Public Housing Conference in Chicago, describing the veterans 'who watched American supplies pouring ashore on the Normandy beaches . . . who saw the endless waste of war. Is it any wonder that [he] cannot understand why he is not housed?' Later, when the first session of the Eightieth Congress came to a close, he expressed bitterness at the lack of action on the bill: 'When they ask me if I was able to get them any homes, I will have to answer "Not a one – not a single one!"'

As a member of the Education and Labor Committee, Kennedy faced a major effort by the Republican majority to replace the Wagner Act of 1935, which they saw as giving unions too much power. But the proposal for a new labor law by the House Republicans, the Hartley Bill, Kennedy perceived as favoring management. In mid-April he made a report that called for moderation, an attempt to balance the power of unions and business. But Kennedy recognized that no one was likely to take his views seriously, not even his father. Joe Kennedy was very much in favor of the Hartley Bill.

A few days after the House vote supporting the Hartley Bill, 308 to 107, Jack and Richard Nixon were asked to debate the issues at a meeting in Pennsylvania. Nixon was to write later, in his book *Six Crises*: 'I was for the bill. Kennedy was against it . . . neither he nor I had even the vaguest notion at the time that either of us would be a candidate for President 13 years later.'

The final bill, renamed the Taft-Hartley Bill, was resubmitted several times through the House and Senate. President Truman vetoed it once. Each time it came to Kennedy, his vote remained 'Nay.' This was his first definite liberal stand, but in the end the Taft-Hartley Act became law.

The first session ended in late July 1947. Since January Kennedy had been traveling back and forth to Massachusetts almost every weekend, not so much to take care of his constituents – he depended on an efficient staff for that – but to give speeches. Although it has been reported that he did not really want the job of Congressman, he was hard-working and kept well-informed. On the social side, popular as a guest, as a host and as a date, he was considered one of the most eligible bachelors in Washington.

In September Kennedy flew to Ireland for a fact-finding tour on European labor problems relating to communism. He stopped off to see his sister Kathleen, who was living in England, and became sick; he was hospitalized at the London Clinic. This illness was reported at the time to be a recurrance of malaria, but doctors discovered a far more serious problem – malfunctioning adrenal glands. In its most serious form this condition is called Addison's Disease, which is incurable, but treatable. Without cortisone or corti-sone-type medication, it could be fatal. Whether or not Kennedy had this conditon is still being debated. However, in 1947 he was apparently so sick that he was given the last sacraments of the Roman Catholic Church. Subsequently, with cortisone treatment he recovered enough to be sent home.

This was the beginning of a controversy that would stalk Jack Kennedy and his family even after his death: the conflict between a patient's right to privacy and the public's right to know the truth about the health of a person in public life. The Kennedys had a precedent for the protection of a patient's privacy in the case of Rosemary, their retarded daughter. In their son's case, what appeared later to be secrecy may well have begun out of fear or uncertainty of diagnosis, with the desire for a second opinion in the United

Opposite top: *The Kennedy family was well known in Boston for its philanthropies, which included the children's home named for Joseph P Kennedy Jr, here being dedicated in 1949.*
Top right: *Rose Kennedy greets guests and coworkers at one of the numerous gatherings where she acted as hostess for her son. Jack Kennedy's ability to get out the female vote was decisive in his 1952 bid for Lodge's Senate seat. As Lodge observed ruefully, 'It was those damn teas that killed me.'*
Right: *Lodge congratulates his successor after the 1952 Senate race (in 1916, Kennedy's grandfather Fitzgerald had run against Lodge's father and lost). The 'lace curtain' Irish had come a long way in Boston politics.*

States. Whatever the reason, the press was informed at the time that Kennedy had malaria. He was put on a regimen of medication that he would have to continue for the rest of his life to keep the adrenal malfunction under control. The fact that his illness had not been clearly identified would become a raging political issue in 1960.

The cover story of Kennedy's 'malaria' was accepted, and he was elected to the House of Representatives twice more. His voting record and political posture continued to defy labels. He was called a 'reservationist,' someone without solid convictions, but he claimed to think in terms of the needs and views of his constituents. Many of his Democratic colleagues criticized what they saw as a narrow range of vision that took in only his own district.

A conspicuous problem in understanding how Kennedy stood on issues was the role of his father in his life. It was no secret that Joseph Kennedy had been the principal force behind the successful election campaigns of his son. There was also a certain amount of skepticism about whether the younger Kennedy could be independent of his father's wealth. Joseph Kennedy's strong conservatism in domestic policies and isolationism in foreign policy troubled many liberals. But his son's political philosophy was still developing, and he continued to deny that his father's views were his own: he insisted that he disagreed with his father, amiably, on most major issues. It was typical of Jack Kennedy that he would also defend his father's role in teaching his children that they should 'determine their own lives and make their own decisions.'

Meanwhile, the Kennedys had been struck by loss again when Kathleen was killed in a private aircraft accident in 1948. Robert Kennedy finished at Harvard that same year and began working toward political life, as his brother had done. The family remained close. Congressman Kennedy was already preparing, during his years in the House of Representatives, for his next move up the political ladder. In the spring of 1952 *The New York Times* carried this item under dateline Boston, April 6: 'Representative John F. Kennedy, Democrat of Massachusetts, announced tonight that he would be a candidate for the Senate seat now held by Henry Cabot Lodge Jr., national chairman of General of the Army Dwight D. Eisenhower's Presidential campaign.'

Kennedy's opposition to Lodge must have seemed appropriate to his family: in 1916 Honey Fitz had run against the first Henry Cabot Lodge and lost. The Kennedys were ready this time, with an organization and an effort as massive as the one which first put Jack Kennedy into Congress. Lodge had as much going for him as his adversary did – wealth, good looks, a Harvard education, war service and a family background in politics. The difference was that he didn't have Joe Kennedy on his side, master-minding his campaign. In November 1952, although Eisenhower won by a landslide, Lodge lost to Kennedy by 70,737 votes.

During the campaign, Kennedy had begun a serious courtship of Jacqueline Bouvier, the daughter of a Wall Street financier, John V Bouvier III. Her

mother, who had remarried, was Mrs Hugh D Auchincloss. Debutante of the Year at 18, Jacqueline Bouvier had been educated at Vassar and the Sorbonne, and was about to graduate from George Washington University.

With Kennedy in Massachusetts on the campaign trail, their courtship was 'spasmodic,' as Mrs Kennedy described it later. But once in office, Jack pursued her in earnest. There was widespread interest in their glamorous Newport, Rhode Island, wedding on 12 September 1953, where 3000 gate-crashers had to be turned away. The beautiful 24-year-old society girl and the 36-year-old Senator were married by Arch-

Main picture: *The wedding of John F Kennedy and Jacqueline Bouvier in Newport, Rhode Island, 12 September 1953. Robert F Kennedy was his brother's best man, and Archbishop Cushing traveled from Boston to celebrate the nuptial Mass.* Top: *The newlywed Kennedys leave the church for their wedding reception at the Bouvier home, Hammersmith Farm; 1200 guests attended.* Above: *Jacqueline Kennedy was working for the Washington Times-Herald as a photographer when she met her future husband in 1952.*

bishop Richard Cushing of Boston, with Robert Kennedy as his brother's best man. After the reception, attended by 1200 guests, they left for a honeymoon in Acapulco.

Left: *Senator Joseph R McCarthy (standing), chairman of the Senate Subcommittee on Investigations that was widely denounced as a 'witch-hunt.' McCarthy led its indiscriminate attacks on State Department officials and others it alleged to be Communists. Robert F Kennedy served on this committee as a counsel, until McCarthy's excesses alienated him from the Wisconsin senator.*
Below: *During the early 1950s, Kennedy's recurring back problem made it necessary for him to campaign on crutches.*

As a senator, Kennedy applied most of his effort to problems of his region, sponsoring bills to help industry there and continuing his stance of moderation and compromise. This avoidance of controversy would lead to a popular joke about Kennedy: 'A little less profile and a little more courage, please.' The bitter joke was brought about by a dispute that compelled national attention during the early 1950s: Republican Senator Joseph R McCarthy's accusation that the State Department was being infiltrated by Communists. In his position as chairman of an investigation subcommittee of the Government Operations Committee, the Wisconsin Senator shocked many by his attacks on the civil liberties of those he was investigating, but others were gratified by his anti-Communist stand. Jack Kennedy had avoided becoming involved in the controversy, which was made difficult by the fact that his brother Robert, through the influence of their father, had become an assistant counsel on the McCarthy staff. When the Senate finally decided to censure McCarthy for what it considered his excesses, Jack Kennedy was in the hospital and unable to vote.

During the last months of the 1954 Congressional session, his back problem had flared up again, becoming so painful that he had to use crutches. His doctors advised that a double-fusion operation on his spine could free him from pain, but the complication of malfunctioning adrenal glands created a high risk of fatal infection from surgery. Kennedy agreed to the operation and entered the Hospital for Special Surgery in New York City. On 21 October 1954, Dr Philip Wilson headed a medical team which performed a lubrosacral and sacro-iliac fusion. Afterward, his

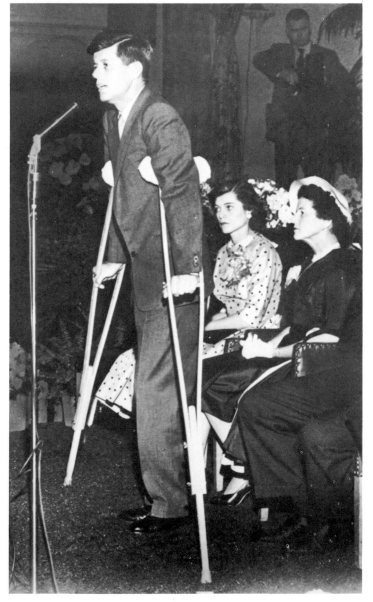

Left: *Senator Kennedy autographs his Pulitzer-Prize winning book* Profiles in Courage *(1955), the story of eight Senators 'who put their nation and their conscience ahead of the political careers and their popularity.'*
Below: *Theodore C 'Ted' Sorenson, who joined Kennedy's Staff in 1953, assisted him in researching* Profiles in Courage *and became a trusted friend and advisor.*

condition deteriorated to the point where his family was twice called to his side. Then he rallied and was finally well enough to be flown to the Kennedy home in Palm Beach, Florida.

In mid-February 1955, he had to re-enter the hospital for removal of a metal plate that was slowing his recovery. He received again the last rites of his religion, but the adrenocortical insufficiency was corrected; two weeks later he was able to return to Palm Beach.

Kennedy was away from Washington for eight months, depressed by his long convalescence virtually strapped to a board. As he explained it later, he had received a letter from a 90-year-old woman who advised him that to keep his spirits up by staying busy. Thus he decided to write the stories 'of eight Senators who put their nation and their conscience ahead of their political careers and their popularity.' The result was his Pulitzer Prize-winning book *Profiles in Courage.* In his preface he gives much credit to his research associate, Theodore C Sorensen, who had joined his staff in 1953. Ted Sorenson became one of his closest friends and an important advisor in his future political life.

Kennedy's life-threatening health problem was not revealed to the public: all that was known was that he had had a back operation. He returned, limping, to the Senate in May 1955, to the welcoming applause of his colleagues. But because he had failed to deal with the censure of Joseph McCarthy, the quip about 'a little more courage, please' gained currency. He would address the criticism in the days ahead.

Back at work in the Senate, Kennedy fought a proposal to abolish the electoral college, worked on

civil rights legislation favoring moderation and in 1957 was assigned to the powerful Foreign Relations Committee, where he advocated economic aid to underdeveloped areas in Africa and Asia. One of the most difficult decisions made as a Senator was his vote for the St Lawrence Seaway. In a 1952 campaign pledge, he had promised to oppose it, but his views on the benefit it would bring to the United States changed his mind – and created the perception that he had gained in political stature. The result was that John F Kennedy was considered a possible vice-presidential candidate in 1956.

Traditionally, the presidential candidate picks his own running-mate, and Kennedy supporters were pressing his cause as Adlai Stevenson's choice. During this campaign the subject of a distinctly Roman Catholic vote became important to Kennedy, and Theodore Sorensen wrote a memorandum known

Top: *Boston businessmen Sherman Whipple Jr, Herbert Evans, Ernest Henderson and Ralph Birney discuss the St Lawrence Seaway with Kennedy before his election.*

Above: *With Adlai Stevenson, who considered Kennedy as a vice-presidential running mate in 1956. However, the delegates chose Senator Estes Kefauver by a narrow margin.*

as the Bailey Report whose statistics were used to demonstrate that a Catholic candidate could help, not harm, a ticket.

The convention opened in Chicago on 13 August 1956. Both the weather and the politicking were hot. Jacqueline Kennedy, expecting her first child, was present in the hope that her husband would be nominated. However, Stevenson threw the nomination open to the delegates. Although the vote for the popular Jack Kennedy was close, the nomination went to Senator Estes Kefauver. Later, when Stevenson lost the election, Kennedy forces were glad their man had not been on the ticket.

Not long after the convention, the Kennedy's first child, a girl, was stillborn. Because Jack Kennedy had been away from home when it happened, rumors began circulating that the marriage was in trouble. The birth of Caroline Bouvier Kennedy a year later, on 27 November 1957, helped to diminish the rumors.

Kennedy's attempt to gain the vice-presidential nomination had brought him to national attention. After the 1956 convention, it was clear to all who knew him that he would no longer be satisfied with any goal less than the presidency. Everything else would be a step along the way. One of those steps, he decided in 1958, was to be elected for a second term in the Senate with the largest possible vote, which would demonstrate his popularity and prove his stature as a possible presidential candidate two years later. His campaign was fought with the usual rich and powerful Kennedy organization. Critics claimed that he was lacking in 'maturity' and 'courage,' and implied that he had not written *Profiles in Courage* himself. But the real feeling seemed to be resentment of the wealth behind him. Despite these charges, he was re-elected to the Senate in 1958 by a margin of 874,608 votes. Massachusetts had never seen such a victory, and Kennedy's hopes as a Presidential aspirant were strengthened.

The Kennedy political organization had long since learned that a successful campaign does not begin a few months before an election: in 1959 the presidential effort began in earnest. One important requirement for his campaign, Kennedy believed, was an identity that would differentiate his position on issues from those of his rivals. The national trend had been basically conservative for some years, but the swing seemed to be now toward a liberal approach. Although Kennedy would insist that he remained a moderate Democrat in political philosophy, he began during this period consistently to support liberal positions on public welfare and civil liberties. Personal publicity was another important part of the campaign strategy: photographs of Jack and 'Jackie' Kennedy appeared on many magazine covers. There were numerous articles on the attractive young couple. And the steady flow of speeches left no doubt that Kennedy was planning to go for the highest office in the land.

On 2 January 1960, Senator Kennedy declared his candidacy for President of the United States. His preconvention strategy was made clear when he announced that he would fight it out in the primaries. By May he had stormed successfully through seven Democratic preferential primaries. In June he spoke to the Textile Workers Union on what would become one of his major themes – the decline of the United States as a world power. The question of his Catholicism came to the fore again, but after continued controversy, he declared at a convention of newspaper editors: 'I am not the Catholic candidate for President.' His critics suggested that perhaps he was the one who was keeping the religious issue alive for political profit.

Top: *Kennedy (left) prepares to 'Face the Nation' on TV.* Center: *TV appearances grew more frequent as it became apparent that Kennedy came across well in that medium.*

Above: *A South African group visits Senator Kennedy. Black leaders in the United States were skeptical about his commitment to civil rights.*

Above: *Strong support for Kennedy's nomination as vice-president in 1956 encouraged him and his supporters, despite the narrow loss to Kefauver. Kennedy garnered national attention at the Democratic Convention.*

Right: *Kennedy announces his candidacy for President of the United States.*

Opposite top: *Powerful Texas Senator Lyndon B Johnson was Kennedy's major rival for the 1960 Democratic presidential nomination.*

On 4 July 1960, Kennedy held a televised press conference to reply to some of the charges of his critics, among them the matter of his youth and inexperience. In his defense, he stated that the demands placed on a President required 'the strength and health and vigor of young men.' Supporters of Senator Lyndon B Johnson, one of Kennedy's rivals for the nomination, concluded that their opponent was alluding to the heart attack that their candidate had suffered in 1955. In rebuttal to what was seen as a 'health issue,' Texan John B Connally, director of Citizens for Johnson, told the press that Kennedy was a victim of Addison's Disease, the most serious form of adrenal disorder. Rumors had been circulating for some time that Kennedy had Addison's Disease, but

this had been denied, even by the candidate himself. Another Johnsonite quoted doctors in communication with the Boston clinic where Kennedy had been treated for many years as saying that he 'would not be alive were it not for cortisone.' But even his opponents would admit that this health problem in itself was not the issue, since a patient could manage very well with medication; it was the lack of disclosure that was troubling. Kennedy continued to deny that he had anything more than a 'partial adrenal insufficiency.' And this, at least, if not the complete disclosure his rivals might have desired, was reported in the press.

Typically, the Kennedy organization did not allow this controversy to stand in its way. It went on fighting with familiar intensity, never taking anything for

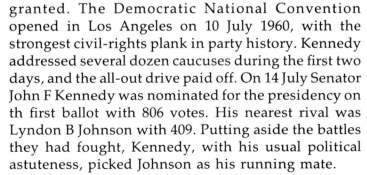

granted. The Democratic National Convention opened in Los Angeles on 10 July 1960, with the strongest civil-rights plank in party history. Kennedy addressed several dozen caucuses during the first two days, and the all-out drive paid off. On 14 July Senator John F Kennedy was nominated for the presidency on th first ballot with 806 votes. His nearest rival was Lyndon B Johnson with 409. Putting aside the battles they had fought, Kennedy, with his usual political astuteness, picked Johnson as his running mate.

The Kennedy-Johnson election campaign was a study in political professionalism. For the nation, the highlight was the series of four face-to-face television debates between Kennedy and the Republican candidate, Richard M Nixon. The first, in Chicago on 26 September, centered on the economic growth of the

Opposite top and bottom: *On the campaign trail in Louisiana and North Carolina – 1960. Poised and attractive, Jacqueline Kennedy was a distinct asset in her husband's campaign.*
Above: *The president-elect greets Nixon in Florida after the November elections.*
Left: *One of the four televised Kennedy-Nixon debates.*

nation and how to maximize it. Although attention seemed to focus on the appearance of the candidates, the debate was hailed as successful. Three more followed, with the men arguing the problem of defending Quemoy, an island off the Chinese mainland, labor problems, nuclear testing and other topics. Kennedy came out looking like a winner and his advisers suggested a fifth debate, but Nixon declined. The medium was less kind to the Republican candidate.

On 8 November 1960, John F Kennedy of 122 Bowdoin Street, Boston, went to the polls and cast his vote, then flew to Hyannis Port to wait for the returns. During the long night he saw that a squad of Secret Service men had been placed around the house. The next morning Kennedy knew he had been elected, but

it was in the Electoral College, with the help of Johnson's appeal in the South, that the vote had been decided. There the margin was 303 to 219. The popular vote was extremely close – Kennedy's 34,227,096 votes to Nixon's 34,108,546. This was considered the smallest mandate in American history.

Kennedy went out to find his wife, Jacqueline, who was walking along the beach. (She was soon to give birth to their first son, John Jr, on 25 November.) They went to the Hyannis armory, where Kennedy gave a short speech, accepting his election as president, pledging to advance 'the long-range interests of the United States and the cause of freedom around the world.' Joseph P Kennedy's dream of having a son in the White House was coming to fruition: the nation waited to see how John F Kennedy would fulfill it.

'Ask What You Can Do...'

Kennedy's first year in office
was recorded tirelessly by the
press corps, seen here on the
occasion of an October
meeting with William Tubman
(seated left), President of
Nigeria.

The changeover of presidential power began on a morning that had been marred by an overnight blizzard and subfreezing temperatures, but by 12:51 PM on 20 January 1961, a bright winter sun was shining. John Fitzgerald Kennedy raised his right hand: 'I do solemnly swear . . .' He had become the 35th President of the United States, the youngest man ever to assume that office by election.

The windswept, flag-draped inaugural platform was filled with the great and famous of the nation. One familiar figure was Dwight D Eisenhower, the oldest man ever to occupy the White House, who was now leaving it. Another was Joseph P Kennedy, watching his son culminate the struggles and ambitions of three generations of Kennedys in the United States. The ceremonies had begun with a Marine Band

Opposite: President-elect Kennedy confers with President Dwight D Eisenhower shortly before taking office.

Before the inauguration of 20 January 1961, President Eisenhower greets his successor and Mrs Kennedy.

rendition of 'America the Beautiful'; contralto Marion Anderson sang 'The Star Spangled Banner'; Boston's Richard Cardinal Cushing delivered a 20-minute-long invocation. As the prayer went on, smoke was seen drifting up around the cardinal at the lectern. As the prayer ended, a group including Richard Nixon dashed to the rescue. A short circuit was found in some equipment, wires were disconnected and the ceremony went on.

Lyndon Baines Johnson took the oath as vice-president, administered by fellow Texan Sam Rayburn. Then 86-year-old New England poet Robert Frost, his white hair stirred by the wind, began to read a newly written preface to his poem 'The Gift Outright.' He faltered momentarily when the sun glared on his paper, but he soon left off reading to recite from memory 'Such as we were we gave ourselves outright . . . .' Kennedy moved forward to stand beside Chief Justice Earl Warren. He placed his hand on a Kennedy family Douay Bible and repeated his oath. His administration was to last 1037 days. As Sam Rayburn was to observe, he had become 'a man of destiny.'

President Kennedy's inaugural address was both eloquent and memorable. He stood before the Capitol, handsome and youthful at 43, calling for a fresh spirit in national life: 'Let the words go forth from this time and place, to friend and foe alike, that the torch has been passed to a new generation of Americans.'

Aware that the nation's domestic problems were intertwined with international affairs, he called on his fellow citizens 'to bear the burden of a long twilight struggle, year in and year out . . . against the common

Opposite: *President Kennedy delivers his inaugural address to a responsive audience that includes thousands of young people attending their first inauguration – that of the youngest president since Teddy Roosevelt. Kennedy called on his countrymen to take part in 'a struggle against the common enemies of man: tyranny, poverty, disease and war itself.'*
Below: *Chief Justice Earl Warren administers the oath of office, which Kennedy took on his family Bible.*

Top: *The swearing-in of the Kennedy Cabinet, including the president's brother Robert (fourth from left) as Attorney General.*

Above: *The return of captured USAF pilots Captains Freeman B Olmstead and John R McKone from the USSR to Andrews Air Force Base: 29 January 1961.*

Above: *Arriving at the extravagant Inaugural Ball, staged by Frank Sinatra. The president called it 'an ideal way to spend an evening' and stayed until 3:00 AM.*

Opposite top; *Union labor opposed Bobby Kennedy's appointment as Attorney General because of his role in the 1957 Senate Labor Rackets Committee, on which he had served with his brother.*

enemies of man: tyranny, poverty, disease and war itself.' With confidence he declared: 'In the long history of the world, only a few generations have been granted the role of defending freedom in its hour of maximum danger. I do not shrink from this responsibility – I welcome it ... The energy, the faith, the devotion which we bring to this endeavor will light our country and all who serve it – and the glow from that fire can truly light the world. And so my fellow Americans, ask not what your country can do for you – ask what you can do for your country.'

His program was called the New Frontier. One of his first tasks had been the selection of a Cabinet to represent it. His choice, bipartisan and based on ability, included Republicans Robert S McNamara as Secretary of Defense and C Douglas Dillon as Secretary of the Treasury. Dean Rusk, head of the Rockefeller Foundation, was brought in as Secretary of State. Texan John Connally, who later would share a sad role in Kennedy's life, was at first Naval Secretary, but later resigned to become Governor of his state. Adlai Stevenson was appointed Ambassador to the United Nations. Kennedy appreciated people 'who can do things,' not just theorize without offering alternatives.

One of Kennedy's most controversial choices, and difficult for him to make, was the appointment of his brother Robert as Attorney General. Besides the probable charge of nepotism, there was his brother's youth (35), and the animosity of union labor toward Robert Kennedy because of his part in the investigation of labor rackets. However, the new president wanted to have someone close to him whom he could trust completely, and 'Bobby' Kennedy filled that need. Another appointment affecting him on a personal level was that of Dr Janet Travell, an expert on spinal disorders and the treatment of pain, as his personal physician.

On the day of his inauguration, Kennedy received a cordial telegram from Soviet Premier Nikita Khrushchev: 'Dear Mr. President, we congratulate you upon your inauguration. We avail ourselves of the opportunity to express the hope that we shall attain a radical improvement of relations between our countries.' Khrushchev made another gesture toward relaxing cold-war tensions between the US and the USSR when he offered to free two American fliers who had been shot down over the open sea and imprisoned as spies – if Kennedy would not make political capital of their release. Jack Kennedy, who now preferred to be known as JFK, agreed, and in his first press conference announced that 'Captains Freeman B Olmstead and John R McKone, members of the crew of the USAF RB-47 aircraft who have been held by Soviet authorities since July 1, 1960, have been released by the Soviet government and are now en route to the US.' Hoping that Khrushchev was sincere in his expressed desire for improved relations with the US, the new President asked somewhat naively if the cold war could be held in abeyance for six months, while the Kennedy Administration got underway. But within five months communist forces had presented threats.

Left: *FBI Director J Edgar Hoover, with whom both Kennedys had an uneasy relationship.*
Below: *JFK took a strong interest in the development of counterinsurgency tactics for use in Vietnam. Here he confers with William Yarborough, of the US Special Warfare Center at Fort Bragg.*
Opposite: *The first official photo in the Oval office.*

Kennedy was usually up by 8:00 AM and moving through his day at a typically fast pace. His personal style was restless and casual. He was a tie-straightener, a sock-tugger. He moved things around on desks. He liked informal meetings, small get-togethers, and breakfast conferences. His working days were long, but when he needed a break in routine, he might take a walk along Washington streets, sometimes with his former Choate roommate, LeMoyne Billings, who was by then an advertising executive.

The new president's Oval Office had been repainted white at his request. On his desk were copies of his own books, a Bible and reading on current affairs. Also on his desk was the coconut shell with the message he had scratched as commander of PT 109.

At his second press conference, Kennedy was asked what unexpected problems he had encountered in his first weeks in office. He replied: 'I think the problem is the difficulty in securing a clear response between decisions . . . which affect the security of the United States and having them instrumented in the field. It is easier to sit with a map and talk about what ought to be done than to see it done.'

His appointment list was always full. He would come to his west-wing office every morning loaded down with notes and newspaper clippings. During his campaign he had promised '100 days of action'; in less than 90, this expectation would fail. But now there was a flurry of messages to Congress. Among them, pet proposals – hospital care for the elderly financed by Social Security and a $5.6-billion plan to aid education – would be defeated.

Early in March, JFK set up a project close to his heart, the Peace Corps, proposed while he was a candidate. He picked Sargent Shriver Jr, the husband of his sister Eunice, as its director. (As someone who knew the Kennedy family was reported to have joked: 'They know their friends and relatives are qualified –

else they wouldn't be friends and relatives.') The Peace Corps was conceived as a plan for specially trained people to aid underdeveloped countries in such projects as road building and health care. The original idea was to enlist only young people, but JFK enlarged the plan to include mature men and women and even older people.

The volunteer response to the idealism of the Peace Corps demonstrated what Kennedy had believed – that many Americans were willing to 'serve the cause of freedom as servants of peace around the world.' Recruitment and training of the first group of 500 began in 1961. This number would increase to 5000 by the spring of 1963, and grow steadily thereafter. Public and Congressional skepticism would be

Left: *President Kennedy greets the Peace Corps volunteers to Ghana and Tanganyika in August 1962.*

Above: *Drumming up enthusiasm for the Peace Corps at the University of Michigan. Volunteer response was all that Kennedy had hoped for and more.*

allayed by this successful effort to promote international good will, although some dictatorships alleged that the volunteers were US intelligence agents. In fact, most of the hard-working Peace Corps members were welcomed in every foreign country where they were sent.

A contest of wills between JFK and Nikita Khrushchev was considered inevitable, and the Southeast Asian kingdom of Laos became Khrushchev's testing ground. There Communist Pathet Lao guerrilla forces were making steady gains in their campaign to take control. Kennedy warned Khrushchev that the United States viewed Laos as a test case for Soviet intentions and that it would not stand by while the country was taken over. For every two guns the Communists sent, JFK declared, the United States was prepared to send three to the pro-Western army of Premier Boun Oum. The United States was serious in its desire for neutrality in Laos, and a cease-fire would be acceptable. Foreign Minister Andrei Gromyko asked for and was granted a conference with President Kennedy, but nothing was said to indicate that the Soviets had changed their position. Indeed, the invasion of Laos intensified.

While Kennedy was still a candidate for president in 1960, anti-Castro exiles known as the Democratic Revolutionary Front had been recruiting volunteers in the United States for a projected invasion of their

Left: *A press conference on Laos, where the USSR tested American determination to keep Southeast Asia free of Communist domination early in the 1960s.*

Above: *The meeting with Soviet Foreign Minister Andrei Gromyko on the Laotian question: 27 March 1961.*

Cuban homeland. They had been secretly trained, primarily by representatives of the Central Intelligence Agency in Central America; financial backing and equipment were provided by the United States. The invasion planners expected that anti-Castro partisans in Cuba would help with a simultaneous uprising, and that the Castro forces would have no air cover. The planners were wrong. Kennedy was briefed by the CIA when he became president-elect, and he reportedly expressed strong doubts that the United States should intervene.

When JFK took office, preparations by the Cuban Brigade of exiles were well advanced. He was finally convinced by CIA reports, approved by the Pentagon, that a landing of the Brigade would result in an overthrow of Castro. On 4 April a poll was taken among his advisers. There were no dissenters, and the president agreed to the plan, with one reservation: he did not want any intervention in Cuba by United States military forces. This was a point of misunderstanding between what the Cuban invasion planners had expected and what actually occurred.

On 10 April the Brigade, composed of some 1400 men, left Nicaragua for Cuba in old cargo vessels. At the same time, eight A-26 light bombers took off for an initial air strike. Within hours, the military headquarters and airports in Cuba were bombed and strafed by the A-26s. Castro immediately accused the United States of being responsible for the attack, but this was denied and attributed to planes flown by defecting members of the Cuban Air Force. This initial air strike did not create the expected massive damage to the Cuban Air Force; thus Castro was left

with adequate air power to counter the invaders when their ships arrived on 17 April. Alerted to the invasion by the pre-emptive air strike, the Cuban dictator rounded up all potential insurrectionists – the fellow Cubans from whom the invaders expected to get support.

When President Kennedy decided to back the invasion, he had hoped the Cuban Communist regime could be destroyed without raising cries of 'imperialism' around the world. But when Castro's accusation followed the first air strike on 10 April, this hope was gone. During the next few days, Kennedy's advisers debated whether or not to allow an air strike using US military forces to cover the invaders when they landed. However, this was seen as a violation of the ban against US military participation. Thus the air strike was rejected by both Kennedy and his advisers, creating a major controversy for the Kennedy Administration after the invasion failed.

Shortly before dawn on 17 April 1961, some 1400 Brigade members made their beachhead on the southern shore of Cuba at Bahia de Cochinos (Bay of Pigs). Meager air cover from their few A-26s offered little protection against Castro's Air Force and Russian-made tanks. Fighting continued for only three days, until virtually all of the Brigade had surrendered.

In Washington, news of the invasion was sketchy, but bleak. President Kennedy followed the dispatches closely, and was at a legislative reception when news of the imminent failure of the invasion came. Hoping to make evacuation possible for the Brigade, he decided to relax his ban and authorized six unmarked

Left: *An unmarked A-26 of the type used by anti-Castro forces during the unsuccessful Bay of Pigs invasion of Cuba (17 April 1961).*
Center right: *Members of Cuba's Revolutionary Army celebrate their victory in a captured launch.*
Bottom: *Cuban Premier Fidel Castro demanded heavy indemnities in exchange for the invasion prisoners seen at center left.*

jets to cover the Bay of Pigs the next day. The jet support was too late. The Brigade had already been overcome.

The disaster that had occurred at the Bay of Pigs was public knowledge by 20 April, bringing disillusionment 10 days before the end of JFK's proposed One Hundred Days. A grim joke spread through White House circles: BC meant Before Cuba. The president made a painful reappraisal of foreign affairs, and the role of the CIA was questioned. However, Kennedy did not avoid personal blame for the Cuban fiasco. In a news conference, he declared: 'I'm the responsible officer of the government, and that is quite obvious.'

In the backlash, anxious to repair the damage, JFK seemed willing to try anything. He felt the professionals in the Pentagon, the CIA and the State Department had failed to provide sufficient information. With a view toward overhauling the system, he appointed General Maxwell D Taylor to head an investigative panel that included Robert Kennedy.

One unfortunate aftermath of the Cuban fiasco came to be known as the Tractors-for-Freedom project. Castro had paraded his Cuban-invasion prisoners through a televised rally and offered to trade them for 500 bulldozers and tractors. A group of private US citizens took up the offer, with the sanction of President Kennedy, although many denounced the proposal as comparable to a World War II Nazi offer to exchange Jewish captives. The deal finally failed in June when Castro raised his demands to an impossible level, (although an exchange was in fact worked out by the end of 1962).

Fortunately, the spirits of JFK and the people of the United States were raised in May by a successful venture. Earlier, in April 1961, the Soviet Union had been the first nation to send a man orbiting around the earth – Major Yuri Gagarin. The secrecy with which it was done made people question the truth of the report. On 5 May 1961, JFK watched a television screen tensely, as a Redstone rocket, carrying Navy Commander Alan B Shepard Jr, lifted off from a Cape Canaveral firing pad and into space. With a smile, the President said 'it's a success.' The choice to televise the liftoff of *Freedom 7* had been Jack Kennedy's, and his confidence in its success had brought back a measure of prestige to the United States.

Soon after *Freedom 7*, Kennedy appeared before Congress for his midyear State of the Union address and asked for a $9-billion program designed to put a man on the Moon by 1971. His request was granted, although it was little appreciated or understood at the time. The institution of the Apollo Program was later considered one of President Kennedy's finest contributions.

Previous pages: *The Kennedys and Vice-President Johnson anxiously await the televised lift-off of America's first manned space flight on 5 May 1961.*
Opposite top: *NASA Astronaut Alan B Shepard Jr is recovered by a US Marine helicopter team after his successful flight in* Freedom 7, *Project Mercury.*
Inset: *Shepard unsuits following his recovery from the space capsule on 8 May 1961.*
Above: *Signing the bill that instituted NASA's Apollo program, shortly after Shepard's historic flight.*
Right: *Commander Shepard is decorated for his achievement: May 1961.*

Kennedy undertook a series of trips abroad in late May 1961. The first was to Canada, where he addressed Parliament to urge Canadian participation in the Organization of American States: 'The hemisphere is a family into which we were born,' he said. Prime Minister John G Diefenbaker made no commitments, but it seemed that JFK had gained some support for his proposals. Later, at a tree-planting ceremony at the Ottawa Government House, he strained his back while spading some soil during the ceremony. It wasn't until he returned to the White House and was tested by Dr Janet Travell that the injury he had suffered became known.

From Canada, Jack went to Hyannis Port to celebrate his 44th birthday. While there, he studied policy papers dealing with the French and the Russians, in preparation for a European visit to Nikita Khrushchev and Charles de Gaulle. The Boeing 707 jet *Air Force One* flew President and Mrs Kennedy to Paris on 30 May 1961. In a motorcade with President de Gaulle, they were taken past the Sorbonne to please Jackie Kennedy, who had studied there in 1950. JFK was satisfied with the conferences he had with the reserved de Gaulle, of whom he reportedly said, 'You know, we do seem to get along well.' De Gaulle himself was quoted as saying that he had met only two real statesmen – Adenauer, who was too old, and Kennedy, who was too young. The French and American heads of state agreed that a firm stand should be taken in West Berlin.

Meanwhile, Jackie Kennedy had become the toast of Paris. The style-conscious city was dazzled by her personal beauty and her elegant entertainments. The cellist Pablo Casals provided an almost historic experience during the Kennedys' first year in the White House. Casals rarely appeared at parties and enter-

Above: *The internationally renowned cellist Pablo Casals makes a rare personal appearance at the White House during Kennedy's first year in office, at the behest of Jacqueline Kennedy. In so doing, he broke a personal vow never again to perform in a country that had supported Franco's regime in Spain.*
Right: *Jacqueline Kennedy with French President Charles de Gaulle during the Kennedys' trip to Paris in May of 1961. Mrs Kennedy's personal popularity there was so great that the president introduced himself at a press luncheon as 'the man who accompanied Jacqueline Kennedy to Paris.'*

Above; *The Berlin Wall, as first constructed by East Germany in the summer of 1961. No Man's Land lies between the fences.*
Left: *Soviet Premier Nikita Khrushchev welcomes President Kennedy to Vienna for a summit meeting on East Germany and other troubled areas. Here Kennedy learned of the imminent peace treaty between the Soviet Union and East Germany, which violated a post-World War II agreement among the Allies.*

tained at this one because of his friendship for Jackie Kennedy. Mrs Kennedy also assumed the task of restoring authenticity to the White House decor, searching through storage areas for period furniture and curios. The White House was to be, she said, 'a museum for our country's tradition.'

After their triumphal stay in France, the Kennedys went on to Vienna, where the president was to meet for two days with Soviet Premier Khrushchev. JFK knew before the summit meeting that Khrushchev would be blunt and tough, but he had yet to learn the extent of that toughness. They reached agreement – on

paper – for a cease-fire in Laos that would soon be violated. When Kennedy asked about the origin of a medal worn by Khrushchev, the premier identified it as the Lenin Peace Prize; Kennedy replied, 'I hope you keep it.' Khrushchev also told him that a peace treaty between the Soviet Union and East Germany was definite, which violated an agreement made with the Allies. JFK's reply was, 'If that is true, it is going to be a long war.' For all his youth and inexperience, Kennedy was able to speak to Khrushchev with a mixture of subtlety and assertiveness that Khrushchev had to admire.

When Kennedy returned from Europe, it was apparent that his back was paining him again. He had to use crutches, and a 'cherry-picker' was employed to get him on board planes. Several consultants were called in, and new treatment was advised, including ultrasonic therapy for his back. The disappointing news was that it would be several months before he could resume any vigorous physical activity.

A treaty banning atmospheric nuclear tests had been under discussion by US, British and Russian negotiators at Geneva during Kennedy's stay in Vienna. After his return, JFK told the nation: 'No hope emerged with respect to the deadlocked Geneva conference. Our hopes for an end to the nuclear tests, to the spread of nuclear weapons, have been struck a serious blow.' Not long after, Khrushchev announced the Soviet decision to test a 50-megaton bomb, breaking a 1958 agreement to abstain from such testing. Continued Soviet tests distributed radioactive fallout all over the world, and fear of the danger of nuclear war spread. After a National Security Council meet-

ing, JFK was grim, but he assured the nation that 'No nuclear tests in the atmosphere will be undertaken, as the Soviet Union has done.' Sales of shelters against radioactivity from nuclear disaster continued to rise.

Khrushchev, in trying to force the West to recognize East Germany as a sovereign state, had threatened to sign a peace treaty there and to turn over control of access routes to West Berlin to the East German regime. In August 1961, East Germany closed all crossings between East and West Berlin. First barbed wire appeared, then a wall through the divided city. The flow of refugees ceased.

Kennedy was firm when he spoke to the nation: 'We do not want to fight, but we have fought before. We cannot and will not let them drive us out of Berlin, either gradually or by force.' He ordered an armored US troop convoy – a token force of 1500 – to travel the autobahn from West Germany through East German territory into West Berlin. If the convoy was stopped, fighting could begin. Next day he learned that the convoy was passing safely through the gate into West

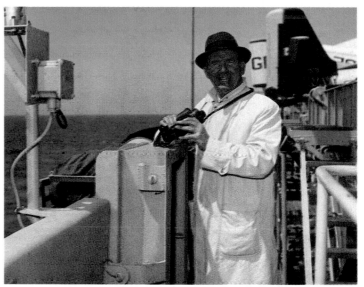

Opposite top: *President and Mrs Kennedy return from Europe to Andrews Air Force Base on 6 June 1961.*
Center: *The historic interview with Aleksei Adzhubei, editor of Izvestia. This was the first interview with an American president published by the Soviet Union's official newspaper.*
Top: *Aboard the USS* Enterprise *during a visit to the Atlantic Fleet at Norfolk.*
Above: *Staff member Dave Powers aboard the USS* Enterprise.
Left: *The burgeoning Kennedy clan at Hyannis Port for Joe Kennedy's birthday – September 1962.*

JFKennedy

Berlin. He was certain now that credibility with the Soviet Union required action.

Other events of Kennedy's first year in office amused or bemused the nation. At the suggestion of White House Press Secretary Pierre Salinger, the Soviet Union's official newspaper, *Izvestia*, published its first interview with an American President. Khrushchev's son-in-law, Aleksei Adzhubei, the paper's editor, conducted the interview. Later, a company in Asheboro, North Carolina, which made the president's oaken rocking chair with a specially curved back recommended by his doctors was astonished by the surge of orders that followed this disclosure.

By the end of the year, the state of the 'New Frontier' economy was on JFK's mind. While the national budget was in preparation, his brother Ted, who was thinking of running for office as US Senator from Massachusetts, called him for advice. He wanted to know how he could face the postal workers whom he would address in view of the veto the President had given their pay raise. 'Look them in the eye,' Jack said, 'and tell them that if we don't get the revenue, we can't provide the raise.'

Early in the spring of 1961, an Inter-American Economic and Social Council had met to draft a plan called the Alliance for Progress. President Kennedy announced that the United States had agreed to furnish long-term development loans providing funds for low-cost housing, education and health programs. Public response to the Alliance was favorable initially, but doubt was expressed after the Bay of Pigs debacle. To dispel disenchantment, a largely ceremonial trip to Latin America was planned. On 15 December the president and his wife flew to Puerto Rico, where banners proclaimed 'Welcome, Uncle Kennedy.' In Caracas, JFK became the first American President to visit Venezuela. His meetings with pro-US President Romulo Betancourt were cordial, and pledges of co-operation within the Alliance for Progress resulted from them. Mrs Kennedy made friends at an agrarian reform project by speaking Spanish to the workers. However, police security for the Kennedys was tight because of threats from radicals.

The Kennedys went on to Bogotá, Colombia, where they were greeted with enthusiasm by huge crowds and a friendly President Alberto Lleras Camargo. At a state dinner, JFK spoke of democracy's unparalleled power 'to meet its new needs without violence, without repression, without a discipline which destroys liberty.'

After his return from the successful trip to South America, the president stopped off briefly in Palm Beach to see his parents. Joe Kennedy, with his granddaughter Caroline, accompanied his son to the airport for his return to Washington. The Kennedy clan was looking forward to spending the Christmas holidays together in Palm Beach, but shortly after his return to the White House, the president learned that his father had suffered a stroke. Kennedy was due in Bermuda for a conference with Britain's Prime Minister Harold Macmillan in less than two days. In the interim, he flew back to Florida, where other family members converged to keep a vigil at their father's side. Before Kennedy left on the military jet for Burmuda, he had seen his father awaken from a semi-comatose state. But Joe Kennedy was still partly paralyzed and unable to speak, as his son's first year as President of the United States came to a close.

Above: *Signing the Alliance for Progress bill in May of 1961. It provided for long-term US loans for development, including housing, education and health programs, in Latin America.*
Left: *A 1961 budget meeting at the Compound in Hyannis Port, which often functioned as a summer White House.*

'A Pretty Good Record...'

British Prime Minister Harold Macmillan wrote to Queen Elizabeth II about President Kennedy that 'He carries the weight of his great office with simplicity and dignity.'

Above: *State of the Union
Address, 11 January 1962:
Congress posed many
obstacles to Kennedy's liberal
programs throughout his
tenure as president.*
Right: *The Kennedy Cabinet,
described as 'the best and the
brightest' by David
Halberstam: on the
president's right is Dean Rusk,
the Secretary of State –
ordinarily the most influential
Cabinet member. However,
Attorney General Robert
Kennedy and Secretary of
Defense Robert McNamara*

*(fourth left) were the strongest
figures in the Kennedy inner
circle.*

Opposite top: *Return of the
delegation to the South
American Punta del Este
Conference of January 1962:
at microphone, Secretary of
State Dean Rusk, flanked by
JFK, Vice-President Johnson
and Senator Wayne Morse.*

As JFK began his second year as president, he expressed a typically wry insight into the situation: 'This job,' he said in January 1962, 'is interesting, but the possibilities for trouble are unlimited.' And indeed the first weeks of 1962 seemed little more than a potpourri of numbers and statistics. His first task was to raise the Regular Army strength from 14 divisions to 16. He approved a balanced budget, contained in 1651 pages, in which $92.5 billion would be spent and $93 billion would be collected. He gave his second State of the Union message to Congress, a speech of 7250 words which took not quite an hour and contained 34 legislative requests. He ended the month by relaxing at one of Broadway's top musicals, *How to Succeed in Business Without Really Trying*.

The premise of JFK's State of the Union message was the close relationship between domestic and foreign issues. The recommendations he made were basically the same as those he had made in his first year in office. Although the second session of the 87th Congress had a Democratic majority, considered essential for the passage of his proposals, most Congressmen still saw his goals as improbable. The business of Congress was conducted with some 250 committees and subcommittees, most of them controlled by a coalition of Southern Democrats and conservative Republicans, neither of whom looked favorably on the issues President Kennedy raised, particularly civil rights. But it was typical of JFK that he would take a pragmatic and indirect approach.

101

Opposite: *President
Kennedy's appointment of his
brother Robert to the post of
Attorney General was highly
controversial and led to
charges of a Kennedy dynasty.
Only Jack Kennedy's
influence with his brother
prevailed over his reluctance
to accept the post. Just before
the announcement, the
president was heard to say:
'Damn it, Bobby, comb your
hair. And don't smile too
much, or they'll think we're
happy about the
appointment.'*

Above: *Leaving the basilica
in Mexico City after Mass,
during a state visit in the
summer of 1962.*
Left: *Touring Mexico's newly
completed National Institute
of Anthropology and History.*

At the beginning of his term, Kennedy had recognized that any strong proposal for civil-rights reform would be defeated in Congress, and that the resulting wrangles would bottleneck every other measure. Thus he had devised what has been called 'the strategy of executive action.' His method was a rapid-fire series of proposals, messages and letters, with frequent news conferences to get his ideas across. He hoped that with an open commitment to civil-rights progress, represented partly by appointment of blacks to government posts, he would gain at least some success. With his brother as Attorney General, the president also expected that the Justice Department would forward the civil-rights movement.

However, Kennedy's greatest expectation in the appointment of a black to office failed in the House Rules Committee in February. Jack had hoped to create a new cabinet post with Dr Robert C Weaver heading a proposed Department of Urban Affairs and Housing. Dr Weaver, then head of the Housing and Home Finance Agency, would have been the first black in a cabinet-level position. The defeat of JFK's proposal was doubly disappointing to him in view of the need, with three-quarters of the nation's population in urban areas, for a department of urban affairs. JFK decided to bide his time on this issue.

Among the problems that President Kennedy inherited from previous administrations was the Powers case. Francis G Powers had been shot down in his photo-reconnaissance plane by the Soviets and had been convicted of espionage in Moscow in 1960. At a news conference on 13 February 1962, President Kennedy announced that U-2 pilot Powers had been released by the Soviets in exchange for a Russian spy, Colonel Rudolph Abel. Abel had been tried and convicted in 1957 as the director of a Soviet spy ring in the United States. In order to free Powers, a commutation of Abel's 30-year sentence was signed by Attorney General Robert Kennedy and President Kennedy.

The next day, Jacqueline Kennedy conducted an hour-long televised tour of the White House to describe the changes that she and her advisory committee had made in the Executive Mansion. Her presentation of White House history charmed some 45,000,000 viewers and increased both the visibility and the popularity of the first family.

Main picture: *A U-2 photo-reconnaissance plane of the type shot down by the Soviets in 1960.*

Inset: *U-2 pilot Francis G Powers, holding a model of his plane, testifies before a Senate committee.*

Above: *A formal portrait in the newly renovated Oval Room of the White House. Mrs Kennedy's improvements to the presidential mansion were justly admired.*

Left and right: *The Blue Room and the Diplomatic Reception Room, as renovated by Mrs Kennedy, who sought to restore the original Neoclassic style of the White House, which had been overlaid by 150 years worth of accretions. To achieve her goal she did extensive research, treasure hunting and borrowing from museums.*

Kennedy's sponsorship of the space program was vindicated again on 20 February, when astronaut Lt Col John H Glenn orbited the earth three times in the Project Mercury capsule *Friendship 7*. When Glenn emerged from his capsule aboard the destroyer USS *Noa* in the Atlantic, President Kennedy telephoned his congratulations. In a national address, the president described Colonel Glenn's achievement as an embarkation on 'the new ocean' of space. The astronaut's wife and three children joined the president on *Air Force One* for a trip to Cape Canaveral. There the president awarded the Distinguished Service medal of the National Aeronautics and Space Administration to Glenn and to the director of Project Mercury, Dr Robert R Gilruth. It was an indirect tribute to Kennedy himself, for it was he who had challenged Americans to reach the moon within the decade.

Opposite: *After the Soviet Union broke the 1958 moratorium on nuclear testing in the atmosphere (1961), Kennedy authorized resumption of such tests in the Pacific and at the Nevada proving grounds. Tactical nuclear weapons evolved from these relatively small-scale tests. Eventually, weapons equivalent to only 250 tons of TNT were produced for battlefield use.*

Below: *President Kennedy's relations with Soviet Premier Khrushchev, seen here at the inconclusive summit meeting of 1961, varied from guarded cordiality to direct confrontation, as in the Cuban missile crisis of 1962.*

If America's race against the USSR in space was a source of satisfaction, another area of competition entailed more somber responsibilities. The Soviet Union had broken the 1958 nuclear-test moratorium with a series of atmospheric tests that began in 1961. President Kennedy announced on 2 March 1962 that unless the Soviet Union agreed to a fully effective nuclear-test-ban treaty before the end of April, the United States would resume nuclear tests in the atmosphere at that time.

The Western European allies approved of the US decision almost immediately; Japan dissented. The Soviet press was critical, and on 6 March, Premier Khrushchev's message to President Kennedy warning that more Soviet tests would follow US resumption was revealed. A joint appeal to the Soviet Union for an internationally supervised ban on nuclear tests was made by the United States and Great Britain on 10 April, but rejected three days later by Khrushchev. With that refusal, the Atomic Energy Commission began its test series (25 April) near Christmas Island in the Pacific. JFK made it clear that he would continue to work for a nuclear-test ban and a Geneva treaty on disarmament.

Above: *Speaking with Lieutenant Colonel John H Glenn after the astronaut had orbited the earth three times in* Friendship 7, Project Mercury *(20 February 1962).*
Right: *JFK and astronaut Glenn confer with Russian cosmonaut Gherman Titov, who pioneered manned space flight.*

Top: *The motorcade to Cape Canaveral, Florida, where the president decorated astronaut Glenn for his flight in Friendship 7.*

Above: *With Secretary of Defense Robert McNamara at the Pentagon, 1962. McNamara's career would soon be enmeshed in Vietnam.*

Above: *John Glenn addresses the crowd gathered to see him honored by NASA's Distinguished Service Medal three days after his historic flight around the earth. His wife and children are seated behind the Kennedys.*
Right: *At the White House, Glenn demonstrates the orbit of his Project Mercury flight for Kennedy, Johnson, and staff and family members (26 February 1962).*

Right: *Addressing members of the International Ladies Garment Workers Union at a housing project in New York City, 19 May 1962.*

Far right: *At Gracie Mansion, residence of the Mayor of New York overlooking the East River, during the same visit to the city.*

In March 1962 the president made his first appointment to the Supreme Court, that of his friend Deputy Attorney General Byron R White as an Associate Justice to succeed Charles E Whittaker, who was retiring. Kennedy had first met White in Germany in 1939, and again when White, known as Whizzer, was a Navy intelligence officer in the Solomon Islands. White had headed the 1960 Citizens for Kennedy Committee during the presidential campaign and was appointed Deputy Attorney General when the cabinet was formed.

In mid-March the President had sent Congress a message on consumer protection. He said that consumers 'are the only important group in the country who are not effectively organized,' and proposed regulatory practices including food and drug controls and a new Consumer Advisory Council. Senator Estes Kefauver struggled to promote the bill, but it faltered in committee and might have failed entirely except for the shocking disclosure of the thalidomide scandal. This new and unproved sedative had been administered in Europe to pregnant women who subsequently

gave birth to infants with missing or stunted limbs. In the United States, the drug had been given experimentally to several hundred people before Dr Frances Kelsey of the Food and Drug Administration succeeded in her effort to prevent it from going on the market. Senator Kefauver now had an object lesson on the dangers of unproved experimental drugs. When the Drug Industry Act became law on 10 October 1962, President Kennedy declared that the consumer now had a law to provide protection from such substances.

On 25 January 1962, Kennedy submitted to the 87th Congress a draft Trade Expansion Act, which he described as 'a new and modern instrument of trade negotiation.' Its enactment, he said, 'could well affect the unity of the West, the course of the Cold War, and the growth of our nation for a generation or more to come.' No other president had possessed the authority to reduce tariffs which this bill, if passed, would give to John F Kennedy. Designed to give the United States freer access to the European Common Market, the bill was feared by many business and union leaders as giving too little tariff protection and de-

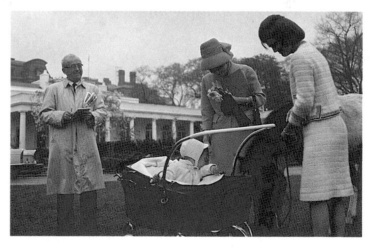

Opposite: *The President and Mrs Kennedy entertain the Shah of Iran, Mohammed Reza Pahlevi, and his wife, Empress Farah Diba.*
Left: *John F Kennedy Jr, whose mother said, 'I don't want my children to be brought up by nurses and Secret Service men.'*

Top: *In Palm Beach for the Easter holidays, 1962: Caroline is four years old, John Jr, 18 months.*
Above: *The Empress of Iran with Mrs Kennedy and her son during the state visit from the ruler of Iran.*

Opposite: *JFK encouraged the children to visit him in his office.*

Above: *Addressing the Golden Ring Council of Senior Citizens on Medicare.*

creasing demand for American products. To counteract resistance to the bill, a nationwide campaign was set up under the Committee for a National Trade Policy. Despite the expected arguments against the measure, the bill was passed with bipartisan support and signed by the President in October. He declared that with the agreements authorized by the act, 'We can move forward to partnership with the nations of the Atlantic Community.'

The fact that JFK had been raised in a family that grew wealthy from business did not make him reluctant to challenge the business establishment. A showdown between President Kennedy and the steel industry came in April, after the Trade Expansion Act. Late in March, labor contract negotiators had reached an agreement between 11 steel companies and their employees, represented by the United Steelworkers, whose contract had been due to expire on 30 June. Under pressure from President Kennedy, negotiations began in mid-February; it was vitally important to him that there be no strike to check economic

growth. Delighted with the settlement reached, he called the negotiations 'industrial statesmanship of the highest order.' His assumption then was that there would be no increase in the price of steel.

The president was informed differently by way of a press release handed to him on 9 April. The announcement that the United States Steel Corporation was raising its prices immediately came from the head of the company, Roger M Blough. The mimeographed press release, which called the steel price rise a 'catch-up,' was given out to newspapers at the same time. Five other steel companies joined the price rise soon after the announcement. The president's reaction to what he considered violation of an agreement made in the national interest was described as 'controlled fury.'

Left: *President Kennedy meets with the Doctors' Committee on Medical Care for the Aged – 27 March 1962.*
Below: *Senior citizens were moved by the young president's concern about medical care for the aging, but Congress posed many obstacles to implementation of his programs.*
Opposite: *The tireless efforts of the Reverend Martin Luther King Jr (inset) on behalf of civil rights for black Americans would culminate in the massive March on Washington – the largest demonstration of its kind in American history.*

Calling what the steel companies had done 'utter contempt' for Americans, the president began a campaign to force them to rescind their price increase. Aside from public denunciation, he had two moves which could be used to convince the companies already involved, and which would help to persuade others to hold the price line. The first was the threat of the loss of government contracts, and the second was criminal prosecution under antitrust laws. Investigations toward these moves were undertaken on 12 April by Attorney General Robert Kennedy and the Federal Trade Commission. On the same day, in a press conference, Roger Blough defended the price increases. However, on 13 April, after two steel companies announced that they would not increase prices, Bethlehem Steel, the nation's second-largest producer, called off its price hike. US Steel followed shortly thereafter. The other companies soon fell in line, giving President Kennedy the victory he had sought for price stability.

The reaction of the business community to the president's victory now included an element of deep distrust. In the midst of the crisis, JFK had been quoted as saying 'My father always told me that all businessmen were s.o.b.s, but I never believed it till now.' Afterward, however, he insisted that he had not been talking about all businessmen – only certain steel magnates. He continued to defend his position as that of the national interest, but those who knew

JFK best suspected that he took a special pleasure in taking on the business establishment.

When Kennedy went to the United Auto Workers annual convention in early May, he was greeted as a great friend of labor: huge signs proclaimed: 'You're the Skipper, Jack, Full Speed Ahead' and 'All the Way with JFK.' His purpose at the convention, however, was to let labor know that he expected the same commitment to staying in line that he had wrung from management. He said in his address: 'I speak as President of the United States with a single voice to both management and labor. I believe that what is good for the United States . . . for the people as a whole – is going to be good for every American company and for every American union.'

Above: *With the Commissioner of Education and official of the NEA, William Carr. Kennedy displeased his Roman Catholic constituency by proposing no aid to parochial schools.*

Kennedy's 45th birthday on 29 May was enlivened by two unexpected events. The first was a pre-birthday celebration – a rally staged at Madison Square Garden at which 15,000 paying guests, and entertainers including Jack Benny and Marilyn Monroe, congratulated the president. The second event, on 28 May, became known as Blue Monday, when the New York Stock Exchange took the worst drop – 35 points – since 1929. The plunge was blamed on everything from a plot to discredit the president to JFK's economic policies. In an effort to reassure the public, Secretary of the Treasury Douglas Dillon issued a statement that 'The general economy is very sound.' Next day, Kennedy received the news that the stock market had made a dramatic turnaround, gaining 27 points above Blue Monday's closing.

In Congress, the president was making little headway with his New Frontier proposals. His unsuccessful effort to launch an Urban Affairs Department was concurrent with the defeat of his 1961 agricultural program, which called for government-imposed controls on production to deal with farm surpluses. His 1962 plan was also replaced by a bill that relied on existing voluntary controls. Other requests to Congress – modernization of the nation's transportation system, an overhaul of unemployment insurance, medical care for the aged and aid to education – were also defeated, despite efforts to enlist public support. On behalf of Medicare, the Golden Ring Council of

Senior Citizens organized a mass meeting in Madison Square Garden to back what was known as the King-Anderson bill. The American Medical Association countered by calling the proposal 'socialized medicine,' and pointed out flaws in the British system as a warning. The King-Anderson bill proposed a health insurance plan for the aged financed by Social Security taxes, whereas the opposition's Kerr-Mills Act provided health care through matching of federal and state funds.

The President's 1961 aid-to-education proposal was adversely affected by the controversy over aid to parochial schools. As a Catholic with a secular education, JFK found himself in an uneasy position. Wishing to avoid the charge of favoritism, he adhered to a strict Constitutional interpretation of separation of church and state, proposing no aid to parochial schools. This disappointed Catholic voters, who had expected more from the first president of their denomination. In 1962, however, defeat of JFK's request for aid to the nation's schools and colleges came from another source entirely – the National Education Association. The NEA contended that government grants to construct libraries, science and engineering buildings in both public and private colleges would imperil 'America's traditional concept of separation of church and state.' With objections coming from both sides, Congress was never able to work out a satisfactory compromise, leaving JFK frustrated in his effort to obtain a comprehensive education bill.

Kennedy's moderate stance on the civil-rights issue was another disappointment to many constituents, who had heard him say during the 1960 presidential campaign, 'If the President does not himself wage the struggle for equal rights – if he stands above the battle – then the battle will be inevitably lost.' His background of wealth and privilege had certainly separated him from most black Americans, but few doubted the sincerity of his belief in the justice of their cause. Once he gained the presidency, however, his critics charged him with standing above the battle.

In 1960, for example, Kennedy had promised to prohibit racial discrimination in Federally assisted housing by 'a stroke of the pen' on an executive order. But his efforts to placate Southern Congressmen resulted in procrastination on this issue. Numerous pens were sent to the White House as a reminder before the President finally signed the order in November 1962.

Another civil-rights case of 1962 admitted of no delays. That fall, a black man, James H Meredith, was to be admitted to the University of Mississippi by order of a Federal court. Accompanied by the Chief US Marshal and a Justice Department official, Meredith had tried repeatedly to register, but had been turned away. Finally, after Governor Ross R Barnett had been

Top: *James H Meredith, whose repeated efforts to register at the segregated University of Mississippi were thwarted by Governor Ross Barnett, until the federal government intervened to stop rioting.*
Left: *Grouped at right, three major leaders of the US civil-rights movement: Jesse Jackson, Martin Luther King Jr and Ralph Abernathy.*
Above: *The racial tensions that had been building since the 1950s erupt into violence.*

J F Kennedy

found guilty of contempt of court, Barnett assured President Kennedy that the state would not prevent Meredith's entry.

Accompanied by Federal officials, Meredith went to the university on 30 September. That night, in Oxford, Mississippi, a crowd of some 2500 students, identified as 'hoodlums' by Attorney General Robert Kennedy, rioted and attacked the Federal Marshals. Some 375 people were injured and two died. The president had tried a moderate approach by an appeal to the Mississippi Governor and to the citizens of the state, to no avail. Now, to quell the riot and to protect Meredith from further attacks, Kennedy had to federalize the National Guard and order 10,000 US Army troops to the area.

The next crisis – arguably the most significant of Kennedy's administration – had deep roots in two problem areas. During the summer, Cuban refugees to the United States had brought reports of a military buildup in Cuba by the Russians, including stories of nuclear installations. On 29 August a U-2 reconnaissance flight over Cuba obtained photographic evidence of a surface-to-air missile site under construction. After receiving the secret report from the CIA, the president decided to warn the Soviets that he was aware of the situation. He went before the nation on 4 September with the announcement that while there was no evidence of 'significant offensive capability either in Cuban hands or under Soviet direction, the United States would use 'whatever means may be necessary' to prevent Cuba 'from taking action against any part of the Western hemisphere.'

Above: *Kennedy's radio-TV broadcast on the Cuban missile crisis was directed as much to the Soviet hierarchy as to the American people: 'I call upon Chairman Khrushchev to halt and eliminate this clandestine, reckless and provocative threat to world peace and to stable relations between our two nations.' Khrushchev would recall later those 'dangerous nights' when 'I slept on a couch in my office — and I kept my clothes on.'*
Right: *The president meets with US Air Force officers after authorizing low-level photographic flights over Cuba: from left, Colonel Ralph Steakley, Lt Col Joseph O'Grady, Major Richard Hoyser, General Curtis LeMay and General Godfrey T McHugh (30 October 1962).*

Left top: *US Navy inspection of the Soviet ship* Volgoles *during the US quarantine – actually a blockade – of Cuba. All ships bound for the island were to be stopped and boarded, effective 23 October 1962. Any ship that carried embargoed material was to be turned away. The quarantine was lifted on 20 November, after the Soviets agreed to remove their war matériél.*
Left: *Missiles en route to Cuba aboard a Soviet freighter. Before the US intervened, the Soviets already had installed a number of 52-foot medium-range missiles on the island. These 1200-mile-range projectiles, equipped with one-megaton warheads, were capable of reaching targets as far away as Washington, DC.*

The Soviets then claimed that they were sending only defensive weapons to Cuba, and that their rockets were so powerful that they had no need of missile sites outside the Soviet Union. They charged in their statement of 11 September that it was the United States that was preparing for an act of aggression against Cuba. President Kennedy had asked Congress for a call-up of 150,000 military reservists. In response, the Soviet statement continued, Soviet armed forces would be raised to peak military preparedness.

In a press conference on 13 September, the President repeated his warning to Cuba and Russia, but also criticised 'loose talk' in the United States about taking military action against Cuba. He was under heavy pressure to take almost any kind of action from a blockade to an invasion. But many urged caution, fearing nuclear war. The president ordered double the number of U-2 overflights; through the first week in October, they indicated that the Russian buildup in Cuba, though large, might be defensive only. On 14 October, however, photographs from a U-2 mission showed a launching pad and ballistic missiles in San Cristobal, Cuba. At this, Kennedy ordered low-level photographic flights to begin on 15 October. These dangerous missions, in which one pilot was killed in a crash, were considered necessary to obtain more detailed photographs. A series of intense secret meetings began, with an ad hoc Executive Committee convening daily. It was estimated that this group had perhaps 10 days to discuss the situation before Cuban-based missiles became operable. Later, the President said, 'If we had had to act in the first 24 hours, I don't think we would have chosen as prudently as we did.'

The President's advisory group was divided between accepting the Soviet missile presence or launching an air strike. President Kennedy held that acceptance was out of the question. Secret military preparations in the Caribbean area began under cover of a planned US Navy-Marine amphibious exercise. When Soviet missiles were first discovered in Cuba, the US had focused an early-warning radar system on the island. Now the US military prepared for a possible invasion of Cuba, the scope of which was later compared to that of D-Day. Alternatives to outright conflict were sought, including a naval blockade to prevent the arrival of additional offensive weapons and to encourage the removal of those already in Cuba. The difficulty was that a full blockade was considered an act of war.

Opposite top: *JFK turns to his closest and most trusted adviser, who gave good counsel on the handling of the missile crisis.*
Opposite below: *An official visit to the 1962 All Stars game in Washington, where the National League beat the American by 3-1. Dodger player Maury Wills scored the first run.*

Above: *When Soviet Foreign Minister Andrei Gromyko (back to camera) met with Kennedy on 18 October 1962, the topic was Berlin, not Cuba – the missile crisis was sidestepped. Gromyko was considered a 'hard-liner' toward the West and lived up to that reputation in several cold-war confrontations.*
Right: *President Kennedy maintained close ties with the anti-Castro leaders of the Cuban Exile, seen here during a 1962 meeting in Miami. The existence of a communist state so close to US borders had been a source of disquiet since Fidel Castro's takeover from Fulgencio Batista in 1959. The CIA-inspired Bay of Pigs invasion (1961) had done nothing to improve US/Cuban relations – or American prestige.*

Meanwhile, the president and his Executive Committee sought to maintain at least the appearance of government business as usual. The president discussed Berlin with Foreign Minister Andrei Gromyko, sidestepping the Cuban missile issue entirely. He spent a few days campaigning to keep up appearances. After 13 days of growing tension, the Executive Committee agreed that a limited blockade, or quarantine, was the most logical approach. Kennedy based his Cuba policy on two propositions: Any Cuban attack on the US would be considered as originating in the Soviet Union, and retaliation would be directed there; also, no further missiles could enter Cuba, and those in place must be dismantled and removed, if not voluntarily, then by the US after an invasion.

On 22 October the President made a televised address to announce that offensive missile bases were being installed in Cuba. His message was presented as a matter of 'national urgency,' and designed as a warning to the Soviet Union. Soviet leaders were accused of 'false statements about their intentions in Cuba.' The President explained that the objective of the United States, via a quarantine on shipping to Cuba, 'must be to prevent the use of these missiles against this or any other country, and to secure their withdrawal or elimination from the Western Hemisphere.'

The next day, 23 October, the Soviet Union challenged the right of the United States to impose a quarantine, and put its own armed forces on alert. US Ambassador to the UN Adlai E Stevenson presented the American position in the UN Security Council. Meanwhile, approval of US actions was given quickly by the Council of the Organization of American States. The president imposed the quarantine at ten o'clock on the morning of 24 October. Missile-base construction in Cuba did not stop, and it seemed the world might be lurching toward nuclear war, as discussions continued in the Kremlin, the UN and the White House. Suddenly, on 26 October, President Kennedy received a long cable from Premier Khrushchev that gave every indication of a desire to avoid nuclear war and to co-operate with Kennedy's formula for removal of the missiles. JFK and the Executive Committee were able to sleep through the night for the first time since the crisis had begun.

Above: *Poinsettias flank the informal dais from which Kennedy welcomed the Cubans of the 2506 Brigade, freed after their 20-month captivity (60 wounded prisoners had been freed earlier).*

Top left: *The 20-month negotiations for release of the 1113 prisoners captured at the Bay of Pigs were finally successful shortly after resolution of the Cuban missile crisis. Freed members of Brigade 2506 were flown to Miami two days before Christmas of 1962, after payment of a ransom of $55 million in food, drugs and cash. President and Mrs Kennedy addressed the group on 29 December at the Orange Bowl.*

Above: *President Kennedy was honored by presentation of the brigade flag for his efforts on behalf of the Cuban exiles. His brother Robert had been instrumental in raising the ransom demanded by Fidel Castrol.*

Right: *One of the silver calendars commemorating the Cuban missile crisis — its dates deeply incised — presented as gifts to key aides and family members in 1963. This one was given to Mrs Kennedy.*

announced that spring that he was running for the US Senate from Massachusetts. At the time, some expressed doubts about the prospect of a Kennedy 'dynasty.' When JFK was asked if he would support his brother's effort, he replied, 'My brother is carrying this campaign on his own and will conduct it that way.' 'Teddy' Kennedy was one of the four Democrats elected to the Senate in November.

By the end of December, President Kennedy had achieved a hard-won objective. For over a year he had been trying to secure the release of the 1113 prisoners, members of Brigade 2506, who had been captured in the 1961 Bay of Pigs invasion. His first attempt with the private Tractors for Freedom Committee had failed when negotiations broke down. But when the prisoners went on trial in Havana at the end of March 1962, a new appeal was made by members of the invasion force who had escaped to Florida. The request to raise the needed ransom was put to Robert Kennedy.

The Cuban Premier finally agreed in early autumn to accept food and drugs as ransom, but negotiations continued on into the missile crisis. This setback was overcome, and a deal was completed. Arrangements were made to raise the required $53,000,000 worth of goods demanded by Castro, who then made a last-minute addition of $2,000,000 in cash for the release of 60 wounded captives earlier in the year. This, too, was raised by private sources. Richard Cardinal Cushing, a Kennedy family friend, was one of those known to have helped in this enterprise.

Two days before Christmas the released prisoners were flown to Florida. The President met with the returned Brigade leaders after Christmas in Palm Beach. A few days later, he went with Jaqueline to the Miami Orange Bowl, not to see a game, but to greet the Brigade, freed after 20 months. He was deeply moved when he was presented with the Brigade flag.

As 1962 came to a close, President Kennedy was asked to review the year's events on television, from his now-familiar rocking chair; newsmen from three major networks interviewed him. He was candid about his own limitations, saying that 'It is much easier to make speeches than it is to finally make the judgments.' But he expressed optimism and confidence in his country: 'If it were not for us, the Communists would be dominant in the world today. I think it is a pretty good record for a country with 6 percent of the world's population, which is very reluctant to take on these burdens. I think we ought to be rather pleased with ourselves this Christmas.'

However, next morning Moscow was broadcasting a completely different message from Khrushchev demanding that the United States remove its missiles from Turkey in exchange for the removal of Russian missiles from Cuba. This was totally unacceptable to JFK. Robert Kennedy suggested that the second message should be ignored – that the original cable should be treated as the only message from Khrushchev. The president sent a reply to the Soviet Premier based on the cable, and on 28 October received Khrushchev's answer. It was, in effect, a Soviet retreat. The President congratulated Khrushchev on his 'statesmanlike decision.'

By the end of November, the Cuban missile crisis appeared to be over. Fidel Castro had refused to allow UN inspection of the missile removal, so the reconnaissance flights continued; photographs showed that the Russians were apparently keeping their word.

As the missile crisis wound down, the midterm Congressional elections were warming up. Some critics suggested that the Kennedy Administration might have invented the Cuban crisis to win the election for the Democrats, but public confidence in the Administration was running high again. This may have helped the cause of Edward Kennedy, who had

'That We May Be Worthy...'

Above: *In 1963 racial tensions boiled over in segregated Birmingham, Alabama. Freedom Marchers demonstrated against discrimination in employment and public services, and were met with violence.*
Right: *Meeting with a task force of Appalachian governors to discuss the 'war on poverty' in the South – 9 April 1963.*
Opposite top: *President Kennedy is presented with the historic Lincoln Letter, a treasured memento of the statesman he most admired.*

At the beginning of 1963, President Kennedy was confident and looked the part. His health was good and he swam twice daily in the White House pool. His working day was long and hard, but he was meeting its demands. Praise for his handling of the Cuban missile crisis was reflected in polls showing that his popularity was high. In his State of the Union message, he sounded a reassuring note on the world situation. The information he had received from US military advisers in South Vietnam indicated progress in the ongoing war against communism in Indochina, where some 56 US soldiers had been killed. JFK told the nation that 'The spearpoint of aggression has been blunted in South Vietnam.'

The President had another kind of war on his mind, which he had identified during his 1960 campaign as 'the war against poverty.' His trips into the South,

including Appalachia, had made him very conscious of the desperate needs of the unemployed, especially black Americans. Although the economy was gaining ground, unemployment figures were still high: if the United States were to maintain its leadership of the free world, it must become stronger economically. His method was a proposed new tax program – a cut of some $13.5 billion in income-tax rates. He expected such a cut to help provide 2,000,000 new jobs a year, higher production, faster growth and eventually a balanced budget.

When Kennedy presented his budget for fiscal 1964, which he called 'frugal,' some members of Congress labeled it 'ridiculous.' With a deficit of $11.9 billion, a tax cut did not seem to be the way to go. However, the President and his advisers continued to pursue the idea that a sluggish economy was the problem, not

Above: *Meeting with a group from the National Association for Mental Health, including Joan Crawford (center), chairman of Stars for Mental health.*
Right: *Presenting an award to Dr. Richard Maseland of the National Association for retarded Children, a cause in which JFK took a strong personal interest.*

Above: *The popular American president received a tumultuous welcome from the residents of Costa Rica, where he went in March 1963 to confer with the six Central American Presidents. Kennedy's backing of the Alliance for Progress was widely appreciated, as was his determination to assist in the containment of communism in Latin America.*

record spending. Their objective might have been achieved had it not been overwhelmed by a related, domestic problem: the most serious race riots in United States history would occur in the summer of 1963. Prior to that came several other measures he had advocated, one of which called on Congress for 'a bold new approach' in the struggle against mental illness and mental retardation (5 February). It was the first bill in United States history to deal solely with the subject of mental health. Community health centers, maternity and child health programs, research centers and vocational rehabilitation would all receive Federal assistance. Although a compromise bill was finally settled upon, the president signed it enthusiastically on 24 October, as a step forward on a cherished project.

Among Kennedy's 1963 proposals to Congress was another Federal aid to education bill, which excluded aid to parochial schools for the third consecutive year. The president still believed that such aid would violate the First Amendment to the Constitution, and his program failed again to get through Congress because of the religious controversy. His views on the relationship between church and state were questioned by Catholics, but his detachment in religious matters was like that on other issues: he described himself as 'an idealist without illusions.'

Cuba was still viewed as a potential military threat, and Cuban-spawned subversion was the subject on President Kennedy's mind when he went to San Jose, Costa Rica, on 18 March. There he spent three days in conference with the six Central American Presidents.

Above: *At the American Embassy with Costa Rica's President after signing the Declaration of San Jose with Central American heads of state. The document called for a Central American Common Market, advance of national development plans and measures to alleviate the problem of exports.*

Left center: *Latin American ties were reinforced by a February 1963 visit from the president of Venezuela, here sharing an open car with President Kennedy. The president's frequent disregard of security precautions was a source of anxiety to the Secret Service men assigned to protect him.*

Left bottom: *In Costa Rica, President Kennedy pledged $6 million in US aid through the Alliance for Progress asserting that 'Economic prosperity is the handmaiden of political liberty.'*

The popular American leader was greeted by crowds larger than the population of San Jose itself, enthusiastically chanting his name to a cha cha cha rhythm: 'Ken-ne-dee! Ken-ne-dee!' In his keynote speech, JFK declared, 'We will build a wall around Cuba – not a wall of mortar or brick or barbed wire – but a wall of dedicated men determined to protect their own freedom and sovereignty.' Economic progress in Central America was a major topic of the conference, and in a signed document the seven presidents agreed to measures which would continue under the Alliance for Progress. When Kennedy returned to Washington, his mood was jaunty. He said at a press conference that the Costa Rican trip had resulted in an agreement on the necessity 'to halt the flow of agents, money, arms, and propaganda from Cuba to Central America.'

During the year-old disarmament conference in Geneva, an unusual agreement had been reached by Khrushchev and Kennedy. During the Cuban missile crisis, it had become apparent that a nerve-wracking amount of time could pass in communication exchanges between the White House and the Kremlin, sometimes as much as seven hours. JFK suggested

Opposite: *With the six presidents of Central America at the US Embassy in San Juan: 19 March 1963.*
Right: *Robert Kennedy and Vice-President Lyndon B Johnson with civil-rights leaders including Martin Luther King Jr, at Kennedy's left, and Roy Wilkins of the NAACP. Wilkins had criticized the Kennedy Administration for a lack of commitment to the civil-rights struggle, observing of the White House staff, 'Not a black face among them.'*
Below: *The violence that erupted against black demonstrators in Birmingham in May 1963 forced President Kennedy to send federal troops into the Alabama city. Weeks later, he made his strongest-ever statement on civil rights, which he called 'a moral crisis' for the nation.*

that a direct line by established – a 'hot line' – and Khrushchev agreed. Kennedy believed that angry words over a telephone might lead to rash action; his choice for the line was a teletype circuit. On 30 August the direct communication link went into operation. Available 24 hours a day, it was to be used only by the heads of state during an emergency.

Although the hot line remained silent, another situation was about to explode that summer, as urban blacks, moved from anger to violence. Washington itself was representative of the problem. In March 1963, it had the highest percentage of blacks in any major US city – over half the population. The increase had come quickly, mainly from the South, with newly arrived blacks looking for jobs, a better education and a better life. What they found was poverty, a neglectful school system and an oppression not much different from what they had left. Young blacks were taking up crime as a way of life. An official in the city was reported to have said, 'We're sitting on a keg of dynamite with the fuse lit.' This metaphor was applicable to other US cities as well.

Two months earlier, President Kennedy had proposed that funds for the District of Columbia be raised

by $47 million. The House of Representative's District Committee, the governing body of Washington (on which JFK had served as a Congressman) was controlled by Southern conservatives who made deep cuts in the proposal. Voter registration drives had been going on in the South for some time, and tension was building as a result. The Kennedy Administration and the Democratic National Committee were urging state legislatures to adopt an anti-poll-tax amendment to the Constitution: the strategy at that time was to encourage and co-operate in Southern registration drives so as to strengthen black civil rights. But blacks were no longer willing to beg or wait for first-class citizenship.

Birmingham, Alabama, had been called 'Bombingham' by blacks because of its history of brutality and violence against them. The demonstrations that began there on 3 April under the leadership of Martin Luther King Jr, were against discrimination in employment and public services and intended to be nonviolent. Over the next month, as the demonstrations increased, so did the arrests. On 2 May some 500 Freedom Marchers, many of them young students, were arrested. When more young demonstrators paraded the following day, violence erupted against them. News and photographs of that violence shocked the nation and the world.

Still attempting moderation, President Kennedy told a press conference that the Federal Government had done all it legally could do, but many disagreed. He was pressing for mediation between black leaders and the Birmingham civil and business community. A truce was arranged on 10 May with an agreement to set up a biracial committee and promises of change in employment practices. But within several days, the violence was renewed with bombings in the black district, including the house of King's brother; a riot followed, in which some 50 persons were injured. The President sent 3000 Federal troops into the area, ready to act if necessary, and prepared to Federalize the National Guard.

Across the country, similar racial battle zones sprang up, complete with demonstrations, retaliations and riots. In late May Attorney General Robert Kennedy met with a group of black spokesmen, but there seemed to be no common ground for discussion. One of their criticisms of President Kennedy was what they saw as his failure to use his prestigious office as a moral forum.

The President and his brother persisted in their use of negotiation and persuasion, meeting Southern businessmen to convince them in terms of economics. But defiance continued. On 11 June Alabama Governor George C Wallace blocked the entrance to the

Opposite top: *Meeting with the US Commission on Civil Rights shortly before the outbreak of interracial violence in Birmingham.*
Above: *An early 1963 meeting with the Committee for Equal Opportunity, chaired by presidential aide Hobart Taylor (at podium). On the left is Willard Wirtz, Secretary of Labor, with Vice-President Johnson seated at right.*
Right: *After Alabama governor George C Wallace refused to register two black students at the state university, JFK federalized the National Guard (11 June 1963) and made an impassioned address to the nation.*

Right: *At the Berlin Wall, 26 June 1963, with West German Chancellor Konrad Adenauer (right). The wall had been built during Kennedy's first year in office, when Soviet Premier Khrushchev exerted pressure on the West to recognize East Germany as a sovereign state. At the time, Kennedy had stated that 'We cannot and will not let them drive us out of Berlin.'*
Opposite: *Chancellor Adenauer greets the president upon arrival in Berlin, where Kennedy spoke to the largest audience he had ever addressed outside the United States. Over a million people gathered in the city's Rudolph Wilde Platz to welcome the popular American leader, who aroused deep emotion by identifying Berlin's citizens with free men everywhere.*

University of Alabama to prevent two black students from registering. When he refused to honor a proclamation signed by President Kennedy, the President ordered Federalization of the Alabama National Guard. Finally, Wallace allowed the students to be enrolled. That night the President went before the nation in a televised address, perhaps the most important one he delivered as Chief Executive. He was responding at last to the demand for a moral forum, and declared the need for an end to discrimination. He said that laws against discrimination 'are needed at every level, but law alone cannot make men see right. We are confronted primarily with a moral issue . . . a moral crisis as a country and a people. It cannot be met by repressive police action. It cannot be left to increased demonstrations in the streets. It cannot be quieted by token moves or talk. It is time to act in the Congress, in your state and local legislative body, and above all, in all of our daily lives.'

A week later the President asked Congress to enact a Civil Rights Act of 1963 which, he said, 'will go far toward providing reasonable men with the reasonable means of meeting these problems.' Various versions of the proposed legislation were introduced

in Congress on 19 and 20 June. While these proposals were being submitted, black leaders conceived the idea of a peaceful march on Washington to convince Congress and the public that blacks were both united and justified in their demands. The 'March on Washington for Jobs and Freedom' saw more than 200,000 people demonstrating peacefully along Constitution Avenue on 28 August in a dignified display of solidarity. Neither the march nor the President's pleas, however, resulted in speedy enactment of the bill: on 22 November it was still bogged down in the House Rules Committee. When it finally passed in July 1964, Kennedy's successor, President Lyndon B Johnson, was the first to recognize it as a tribute to John Kennedy and one of his greatest achievements.

Late in June President Kennedy made a 10-day trip to Europe to reaffirm the US commitment to freedom there. He hoped to dispel some of the friction which had arisen among members of the Western Alliance. His tour of West Germany was one of the political and personal highlights of his trip. Chancellor Konrad Adenauer welcomed him with enthusiasm, and in West Berlin, 100 miles inside communist territory, the streets were lined with tumultuous crowds.

Above: *The president's Irish cousins – Mary Ann, Josie and May Ryan, and Jim Kennedy – welcome him to Dunganstown.*

When Kennedy made his inspection of the formidable Berlin Wall on 26 June 1963, his shock was apparent, as was his respect for the endurance of the Berliners. More than 1,000,000 people had greeted him in West Berlin, and looking out over the huge crowd before the city hall, he spoke with deep emotion: 'All free men, wherever they may live, are citizens of Berlin, and, therefore, as a free man, I take pride in the words *"Ich bin ein Berliner."'*

While in Europe JFK also made a sentimental journey to Ireland to greet his relatives there. On his visit to Italy he had a private audience with Pope Paul VI, who had been named the supreme pontiff only a few days earlier. As successful as his trip to Europe had been, however, JFK returned to America concerned with other matters.

A few days after his visit to West Berlin, he had learned that Nikita Khrushchev had stated willingness to agree to a limited nuclear-test ban. But Khrushchev's agreement was tied to implied recognition of East Germany by the Western powers, which was unacceptable to the United States. The US had first suggested a limited test ban at the Geneva disarmament conference in 1962, but the Soviet Union had turned it down at that time, which stalled negotiations for over a year: not until May 1963 was the subject reopened. On 10 June, before he left for Europe, Kennedy had given a commencement address at American University in Washington, which proposed 'a strategy of peace.' 'And is not peace,' he asked, 'in the last analysis, basically a matter of human rights – the right to live out our lives without fear of devastation – the right to breathe air as nature provided it – the right of future generations to a healthy existence?' He declared that the United States

Top and right. *In Rome (July 1963), Kennedy had a private audience with Pope Paul VI, who would be the first pontiff to visit America.*

Above: *Taking part in a wreath-laying ceremony at Italy's Tomb of the Unknown Soldiers in the capital: 1 July 1963.*

JF Kennedy

Right: *The president signs the instruments of ratification for the Nuclear Test Ban Treaty on 10 July 1963. Soon afterward, he told his friend Dave Powers that this was the happiest day of his life. The treaty culminated 18 years of arms-control negotiations with the Soviet Union.* Bottom right and opposite: *JFK receives an honorary degree from the American University and delivers a memorable commencement address on peace, 'the necessary rational end of rational men. I realize that the pursuit of peace is not as dramatic as the pursuit of war. But we have no more urgent task.'*

would not conduct further nuclear tests in the atmosphere 'so long as other states do not do so.' The Soviet press published the text of this speech, which seemed to indicate a favorable reaction to Kennedy's proposals, and Averell Harriman, who was respected by Khrushchev, was sent to Moscow. Ten days after negotiations began between the United States, British, and Soviet delegates, an agreement was reached; on 5 August a treaty was signed in a Kremlin ceremony. It would not end the arms race, and excluded underground testing, but it did prohibit nuclear testing in the atmosphere, in space and under water.

In a television address to the nation, President Kennedy explained the treaty's significance: 'For the first time in many years the path to peace may be open.' Some 18 years of arms-race negotiations had finally resulted in a treaty. Although the test ban was limited, and would not reduce nuclear stockpiles, the president called it 'an important first step – a step toward peace – a step toward reason – a step away from war.' When the Senate consented to the treaty on 24 September, JFK declared that it was 'a welcome culmination of this effort to lead the world once again to the path of peace.'

JF Kennedy

Below: *The Kennedys arrive in San Antonio, Texas, on 21 November 1963, to a welcome from Governor John B Connally and his wife. Only days before, the president had confided to his friend Senator George Smathers of Florida, 'God, I hate to go out to Texas . . . I just hate to go.' His associates attributed this reluctance to fatigue.*
Opposite top: *A youthful escort accompanies JFK to the helicopter that will take him from Hyannis Port to Washington during his last summer at the family compound.*

Jacqueline Kennedy was expecting her fourth child late in the summer of 1963. Public interest was high, since no child had been born to the wife of a President in office for 68 years. Because of a history of premature births, she gave up most of her official duties, but on 7 August, five weeks before term, she was rushed to the hospital in premature labor. She gave birth to a son, who was immediately baptized Patrick Bouvier Kennedy. Upon arrival at the hospital, John Kennedy learned that his newborn son was desperately ill with hyaline membrane disease, common and often fatal to premature infants. The baby was brought to Children's Memorial Hospital in Boston for radical treatment in a hyperbaric pressure chamber that forced oxygen into the lungs, but he lived only a little over 39 hours. The bereaved president attended the funeral without his wife, who was still hospitalized. On 12 September, the Kennedys quietly observed their tenth wedding anniversary.

146

Left: Houston – the second stop on the ill-fated trip to Texas. Vice-President and Mrs Johnson had joined the Kennedys in San Antonio earlier in the day.

Above: Jacqueline Kennedy and Mrs Johnson with Vice-President Johnson and the Connallys at Brooks Air Force Base, near San Antonio: 21 November 1963.

On 21 November President and Mrs Kennedy left Washington for a three-day tour of Texas. They planned to return by the 25th, their son 'John-John''s third birthday. Jackie Kennedy, who had never been to the Southwest, was looking forward to the trip, but for JFK it was to be a time of fencemending among bitterly split Democratic factions. He had expressed the wish not to make the trip, but this was attributed to simple fatigue.

On their arrival in San Antonio, the Kennedys were joined by Vice-President and Mrs Johnson and proceeded to Houston and Forth Worth. At a breakfast meeting in Fort Worth, JFK was presented with a cowboy hat as a souvenir. The president disliked almost any kind of headgear – which had been something of a political liability when he first ran for office in the hat-manufacturing state of Massachusetts – and he fumbled with the oversize hat for a moment before saying that he would wait until he returned to the White House to be photographed in it.

Above: *The presidential party is greeted warmly by residents of Dallas. Kennedy had been assured that the political infighting in Texas had diminished.*

Opposite: *The arrival at Love Field, Dallas. The speech that the president would never make there warned against 'seemingly swift and simple solutions.'*

Later that morning of 22 November, *Air Force One* landed at Love Field, Dallas, where the presidential party was greeted warmly. An admirer gave Jacqueline Kennedy a large bouquet of red roses, which she carried to the waiting limousine: its top had been removed to provide the crowds with a better view of the President and his wife, who sat in the rear seat. Texas Governor John B Connally and his wife sat on jump seats facing them. The motorcade was to proceed through Dallas to the Trade Mart, where the President would address a luncheon meeting. Secret Service agents were behind the presidential car, followed by the Johnsons' vehicle and a fourth car carrying reporters.

Below: *Onlookers take cover minutes after the president was shot, in this still from a film shot by a Navy cinematographer in the Kennedy entourage.*

Opposite: *On the morning of November 22, the Kennedys were in Fort Worth, en route to Dallas. A motorcade took them to Carswell Air Force Base, where they boarded* Air Force One *with the Connallys. Mr and Mrs Johnson were in the vice-presidential Boeing 707,* Air Force Two.
Above: *Mrs Kennedy speaks to her husband moments before the shots rang out from the unseen assailant's rifle.*

All along the 11-mile route, the motorcade was greeted by enthusiastic crowds. About 12:30 PM, Central Standard Time, near the end of the route, the president's limousine approached an underpass. As it passed the Texas School Book Depository Building, three shots rang out in rapid success. President Kennedy was first struck from the back, in his right shoulder. Another bullet tore into the back of his head. Governor Connally was seriously wounded, apparently by the second shot.

President Kennedy collapsed on his wife's lap. Holding him in her arms, she cried out 'Jack! Jack! Oh, no!' She struggled toward the back of the car to help in a Secret Service agent who had been on the running board of the following car. Too late, he shielded the president and his wife with his body.

The presidential car raced to Parkland Hospital, five minutes away. There a team of surgeons worked desperately to save Kennedy, but hospital officials said later that he was 'medically dead' on arrival in the emergency room. Catholic priests administered last rites. This time there would be no reprieve.

Across the country, family members learned the appalling news. In Hyannis Port, Rose Kennedy delayed telling her husband of his son's death until his physician could advise whether he was strong enough to sustain the shock. Edward Kennedy revealed it to his father the following morning. Caroline

Left: *Immediately after the shooting, President Kennedy slumps in the back seat of his black Lincoln, as his wife cries 'Oh, no!' Secret Service agent Clinton Hill leaps onto the bumper, then into the car, which speeds toward Parkland Memorial Hospital. Governor Connally, too, had been wounded, but not mortally.*

and John Kennedy Jr were too young to comprehend the finality of death, but they, too, had to be told. Media attention was focused totally on Dallas, and millions abandoned their everyday pursuits to follow the events unfolding there.

About two hours after the assassination, the president's body was put aboard *Air Force One* for the sad return to Washington. Before the plane left Love Field, Vice-President Lyndon B Johnson took the oath of office as 36th President of the United States. One of the witnesses was Jacqueline Kennedy, in her blood-stained pink wool suit. As the plane flew across the country, the new president conferred with the government officials on board to ensure a smooth transition. One of Johnson's first presidential acts was to designate the day of John F Kennedy's funeral as a national day of mourning.

About the same time that *Air Force One* was leaving for Washington, Dallas police were arresting the suspected killer, 24-year-old Lee Harvey Oswald, a former expatriate to the Soviet Union. Three miles from the crime scene, Oswald had shot and killed a police officer who had noticed his suspicious behavior. He was caught soon after and charged with having shot Kennedy and Connally from the sixth-floor window of the Texas School Book Depository. Evidence said to be conclusive linked Oswald with the two murders. Shortly after the President was shot, an Italian carbine and three empty shells had been discovered at the alleged site of the shootings. Police traced the carbine to a Chicago mail order house,

which had sent it to a Dallas post office box addressed to 'A Hidell.' The evidence included fingerprints, ballistic tests of the carbine, the name A Hidell, and the post box number, found among Oswald's possessions.

On 24 November, the accused assassin was moved from the Dallas Police Headquarters to the county jail. In view of millions via television, he was shot in a

Above and far left: *Lyndon B Johnson is sworn in as the thirty-sixth president of the United States by Judge Sarah Hughes aboard* Air Force One *after a televised address.* Left: *Shocked residents of the nation's capital gather opposite the White House after news of the president's death flashes across the country.*

basement pasage by a Dallas nightclub owner named Jack Ruby. This gave rise immediately to charges of a conspiracy. Ruby was convicted of Oswald's murder the following year.

A week after President Kennedy's death, a special commission headed by Chief Justice Earl Warren was appointed by President Johnson to investigate the assassination and 'to satisfy itself that the truth is known as far as it can be discovered, and to report its findings and conclusions.' Ten months later, the commission reported its findings: both Oswald and Ruby had acted alone, there had been no conspiracy. Many doubted the accuracy of these findings, and speculation about the assassination went on for years thereafter. As James Reston put it, 'What was killed was not only the President but the promise.'

Left: *The flag-draped casket with its Honor Guard in the East Room of the White House: 23 November 1963. The following day, it was moved to the Capitol Rotunda for public viewing. Mrs Kennedy had requested that the funeral arrangements conform as closely as possible to those for President Abraham Lincoln; her brother-in-law Sargent Shriver handled the arrangements, and Cardinal Cushing traveled from Boston to officiate at the funeral Mass on 25 November.*
Below: *Pallbearers from all branches of the armed services carry the casket into the White House.*
Opposite: *Placing the president's casket on the caisson for the funeral procession at the North Portico of the Capitol.*

The immediate reaction, both in the United States and abroad, was one of stunned disbelief. Flags flew at half mast. Schools and businesses closed. Messages of condolence poured into Washington from around the world.

Jacqueline Kennedy's gracious conduct throughout the ordeal earned the world's admiration. On her return to Washington, she requested that her husband's funeral be modeled on that of Abraham Lincoln. Symbolic details of the state funeral were to include the Navy hymn, interment at Arlington National Cemetery, because 'He belongs to the country' and an 'eternal flame' at the head of Kennedy's grave.

The flag-draped casket, first placed in the East Room of the White House, was brought to the Capitol rotunda on 24 November to lie in state for public viewing. A five-service military honor guard surrounded the casket. Brief ceremonies of eulogy were held while Jacqueline Kennedy and her children stood nearby. The public was then invited to file past the bier. Almost a quarter of a million people waited in line to go through the rotunda before the doors were closed the following morning.

Early on 25 November, the casket was placed on a horse-drawn caisson to the sound of muffled drums. The caisson was followed by a riderless black horse on which military boots were reversed in silver stirrups to signify that a commander had fallen. Behind it came the Kennedy family and a cortege that included representatives of over 100 nations, among them eight heads of state and 10 prime ministers. The funeral procession made its way to St Matthew's Cathedral, eight blocks from the White House.

Richard Cardinal Cushing, a family friend of long standing, celebrated a Pontifical Mass in the cathedral, with participants ranging from the White House domestic staff to Astronaut John Glenn, civil-rights leader Martin Luther King Jr, and the hundreds of others who wished to express their grief and respect. At the end of the service, part of President Kennedy's inaugural address was read. As the flag-draped casket was borne out, Jacqueline whispered to her son, who responded with a salute.

The cortege then proceeded to Arlington National Cemetery, where President Kennedy was buried in a site near the Custis-Lee Mansion. Air Force bagpipers sounded their mournful tributes, as 50 USAF jets, representing the states of the Union, overflew the site. A bugler faltered over taps. The flag which had covered the coffin was handed to Jacqueline Kennedy, who then lit the 'eternal flame' at the head of the grave. The funeral was over.

All over the world, John Kennedy was deeply mourned. In West Berlin a band played *Ich Hatt' einen Kameraden* – the dirge of the fallen soldier. In Dallas, people were trying to understand why it had happened, and why in their city. Texas Governor John

Opposite top: *The funeral procession heads toward the National Cemetery at Arlington.*
Opposite center: *The riderless horse at the White House gates.*
Opposite bottom: *Bagpipers sound their mournful notes at the burial.*
Left: *Folding the flag at graveside for presentation to Mrs Kennedy.*
Below left: *The grieving family.*
Below: *Mrs Kennedy would write to President Lyndon Johnson after the funeral: 'Thank you for walking yesterday – behind Jack. You did not have to do that.'*

Connally, recovering from his wounds, said, 'I think we all must suffer for a lack of tolerance . . . which permeates the whole society in which we live and which manifested itself here on Friday.'

As a politician and statesman, John F Kennedy had relied perhaps too much on style and image. He had been only moderately successful in getting the legislation he favored enacted, and some questioned his sincerity in the causes he espoused because of his apparent detachment from the fray. Even his critics, however, would admit that he learned from experience and welcomed good counsel. There was widespread regret that the 'thousand days' of his administration had not provided a sufficient time frame in which to judge the man and his accomplishments.

In the wake of his brutal assassination, the world chose to judge John F Kennedy not on what he had accomplished, but on what he was thought to represent. As Prime Minister Harold Macmillan of Great Britain suggested: 'He seemed, in his own person, to embody all the hopes and aspirations of this new world that is struggling to emerge – to rise Phoenix-like from the ashes of the old.' In this context, history's evaluation of John F Kennedy must include not only the man himself, but the mythical elements that have sprung up around him in response to the traumatic events of his – and our – time.

INDEX

Numerals in italics indicate illustrations

PICTURE CREDITS
The photographs in this book are credited to the John F Kennedy Library, Boston, Massachusetts, with the following exceptions:
Bachrach/John F Kennedy Library: 29 (top)
Choate Rosemary Hall: 21 (below)
College of the Holy Cross/John F Kennedy Library: 10 (top), 11
Philip Drell/Black Star: 73 (below)
Robert Hunt Library: 40-41, 54
Pati Jones/Choate Rosemary Hall: 20 (top)
Library of Congress: 14 (bottom)
Charles Moore/Black Star: 132 (top), 137
National Archives: 41 (inset)
NASA: 90 (both)
Flip Schulke/Black Star: 93 (top)
Stoughton/Lyndon Baines Johnson Library: 153 (top)
TPS/Keystone: 82 (center, both), 104-05 (both)
US Army Photograph: 52, 53 (center), 55 (top), 76, 82 (below)
US Defense Department, Marine Corps: 48-9
US Marine Corps: 49 (bottom right)
US Naval Photographic Center: 42
Werner Wolf/Black Star: 93 (below)
White House Historical Association: 107 (below left and right)

ACKNOWLEDGMENTS
The author and the publishers would like to thank the following people who helped in the preparation of this book: Michael Rose, who designed it; Mary R Raho, who did the picture research with very valuable assistance from James Cedrone of the John F Kennedy Library; Robin L Sommer, who edited it; and Florence Norton, who prepared the index.